TIMELINES IN SCIENCE

A REBIRTH OF SCIENCE

Craig Boutland

ROSEN PUBLISHING

Published in 2025 by The Rosen Publishing Group, Inc.
2544 Clinton Street, Buffalo, NY 14224

Portions of this work were originally authored by Charlie Samuels and published as *Revolutions in Science*. All new material in this edition was authored by Craig Boutland.

PICTURE CREDITS
t=top, b=bottom, l=left, r=right, c=center

Front Cover: Shutterstock: gallimarfry main, Mark C Morris tl, ONYXprj tc, Vadim Sadovski tr.
Inside: Adobe Stock: 17; Alamy: Art Collection 28, 53, Balfore Archive Images 51, GL Archive 29t, Historic Images 52, Logic Images 30, Science History Images 59, The History Collection 23; Bridgeman Images: Christie's Images 61; iStock: Jacus 24, Dariusz Sas 6, Erwin Wodicka 25br; Public Domain: landkaart 20, Lorenzo Lippi 11t, Konrad Miller 21, Museo Galileo 27, Abraham Ortelius 22, Science History Institute 58, Thinkstock/Photos.com 7t, 8t, 9, 18, 19t, 25t, 33, 36, 37, 38, 39t, 45t, 45b, 46, 49, 54, 57; Rijksmuseum: Nederlands Museum voor Geschiedenis en Kunst/Museum Boerhaave 50; Shutterstock: Arogant 7b, Awe Inspiring Images 41, Anthony Baggett 42, Laurent Dambies 16, Janaka Dharmasena 12, 13t, 14r, 15, Dyonna 32, Daniel Gale 55, Philip Ho 35t, Leigh 13c, Lofoto 44, Lolloj 14l, Andrei Merkulov 19cr, Kenneth V. Pilson 10, stock 11b, Triff 5, Paul Van Eykebem 47, Yakobchuk Vasyl 40; Wellcome Images: 31.

All other artwork and illustrations Brown Bear Books Ltd

Cataloging-in-Publication Data

ames: Boutland, Craig.
Title: A rebirth of science / Craig Boutland.
Description: Buffalo, NY : Rosen Young Adult, 2025. | Series: Timelines in science | Includes glossary and index.
Identifiers: ISBN 9781499477702 (pbk.) | ISBN 9781499477719 (library bound) | ISBN 9781499477726 (ebook)
Subjects: LCSH: Science, Renaissance–Juvenile literature. | Renaissance–Juvenile literature. | Inventions–History–Juvenile literature. | Technological innovations–History–Juvenile literature.
Classification: LCC Q125.2 B68 2025 | DDC 509.03–dc23

Manufactured in the United States of America

CPSIA Compliance Information: Batch #CSRYA25.
For further information, contact Rosen Publishing at 1-800-237-9932.

CONTENTS

Introduction

The period from the start of the 16th century to the beginning of the 18th century saw a huge expansion in what people understood about themselves and their world.

The growth of learning had its roots in changes that had begun in the late Middle Ages. Economic growth in Europe brought increased trade, bigger towns and cities, and the exchange of ideas as more people traveled farther. One result was the Renaissance, literally a "rebirth" of classical learning, which spurred a new spirit of inquiry into many subjects. The artist Leonardo da Vinci devised complex machines, while astronomers Nicolaus Copernicus and Galileo Galilei both denied the accepted belief that the sun went around Earth. Their theories were among the many new ideas that circulated rapidly throughout Europe thanks to the development of cheaper forms of printing.

The Age of Reason

The 17th century was dominated by thinkers such as Galileo and the English scientist Isaac Newton. But these men were experimenters as well as thinkers. They used observation and experiment to formulate laws about the workings of the universe that are still accepted today. In doing so, they laid the foundations of modern scientific methods.

About This Book

This book uses timelines to describe the vast upheavals that took place in scientific knowledge from about 1500 to about 1700. A continuous timeline of the whole period runs along the bottom of all the pages. Its entries are color-coded to indicate the different fields of science to which the developments belong. Each chapter also has a subject-specific timeline, which runs vertically down the side of the page.

Advances in scientific methods, including better telescopes and microscopes, revealed unseen details—from the surface of the moon to the shape of bacteria.

Printing

Printing originated in China in about the ninth century. By 1045, Bi Sheng had invented movable type made of baked clay and within 10 years was printing books with it.

Movable type can be made into words and pages, then taken apart and reused.

TIMELINE
1500–1507

KEY:

- Astronomy and Math
- Physical and Life Sciences
- Technology

1500 English printer Wynkyn de Worde sets up a printing press in Fleet Street, London, which establishes it as the city's future newspaper center.

1500

1500 Chinese inventor Wan Hu tries to make a flying machine by tying 45 rockets to the back of a chair; the device explodes, killing him.

1500 Portuguese navigator Pedro Cabral reaches the coast of Brazil and claims it for Portugal.

Johannes Gutenberg was the first European to use movable type.

Timeline

1395 Cast metal type used in Korea

1403 Bronze type used in Korea

1438 Wooden blocks used by Koster for printing

1442 Printing press established by Gutenberg

1455 World's first book printed using movable metal type

1474 First book printed in the English language

The first Chinese printers made paper money and books, with each page of characters carved from a single block of wood to make the printing "plate." The same technology dominated European printing until the middle of the 15th century.

Printing from cast-metal type began in Korea in the 1390s. In 1403, the Korean king Taejong authorized the casting of metal type in bronze. Other printers adopted woodcuts for printing, often carving the type for whole pages out of a single piece of wood. That had the disadvantage that every new page had to be carved from scratch. It would be more efficient to be able to arrange a set of standard characters to

Gutenberg adapted a wine press to squeeze the paper against the inked type.

1502 Death of Italian physician Antonio Benevieni, pioneer of using autopsies to find a cause of death.

1507 The Italian architect Fra Giovanni Giocondo constructs the Pont Notre Dame in Paris to connect the North Bank of the Seine River to the island of La Cité, site of Notre Dame Cathedral.

1502 1503 1507

1502 German clockmaker Peter Henlein makes the first spring-driven pocket clock (watch).

1503 Spanish military engineer Pedro Navarro explodes a series of mines under castles at Naples, beginning a new form of land warfare.

Letterpress Printing

In letterpress printing, characters are raised, mirror-image letters. They are set as text and locked into a frame, then inked with a roller. Paper is pressed against the type. When the paper is peeled off the type, it retains the printed image of the letter.

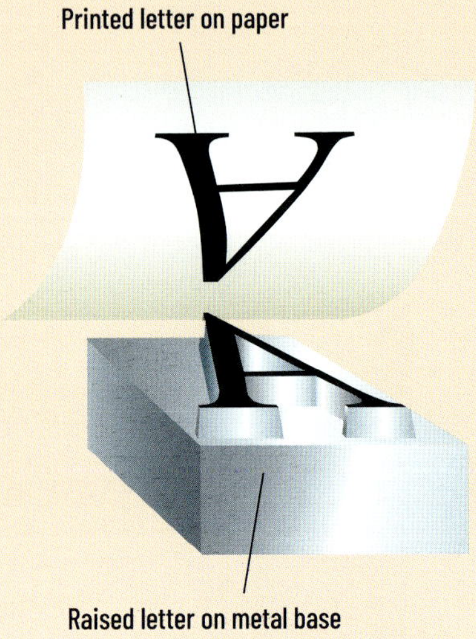

Early pages were highly valuable, so they were bound into protective covers.

form sentences and paragraphs. However, there are thousands of different characters in the Chinese language. In 1313, the Chinese printer Wang Chen had to use more than 50,000 movable wooden characters to print his *Treatise on Agriculture*.

By 1438, Dutch printer Laurens Koster of Haarlem is thought to have used movable wooden blocks for printing. The blocks were far more useful for European languages, which only had 26 characters—the letters of the alphabet—and various punctuation marks, such as periods and commas.

TIMELINE
1513–1518

KEY:
- Astronomy and Math
- Physical and Life Sciences
- Technology

1513 Swiss artist Urs Graf introduces the technique of metal etching.

1513 Spanish explorer Vasco Balboa crosses the Isthmus of Panama and sees the Pacific Ocean.

1515 The wheel-lock pistol is introduced in Germany.

1515 German astronomer Johannes Schöner makes the first globe to include the name "America."

Johannes Gutenberg

Metal type was reinvented in Europe by the German inventor Johannes Gutenberg (c.1400–1468) in the 1440s. Gutenberg brought together the ideas of making copper molds in which to cast the type, a suitable low-melting lead alloy to do the casting, a special oil-based printing ink, and—most importantly—a printing press that would squeeze the paper against the inked printing plates. For this purpose, Gutenberg adapted the screw press, which was already in common use in southern Europe for crushing the juice out of grapes to make wine. (Early East Asian printers did not use a printing press. Instead, they placed the paper on the inked type and used a brush or a roller to push the paper and the type into contact.)

Gutenberg's Bible of 1455 was the first book ever printed using movable metal type.

Gutenberg set up his first printing press in about 1442 in Strasbourg, France, but around 1450 he returned to his hometown of Mainz, Germany. There he established a press using money put up by his commercial partners, German businessman Johann Fust and German printer Peter Schöffer. Gutenberg's first book—and the world's first book ever to be printed using movable metal type—was a Latin Bible, which he produced in 1455 with his new partner, Konrad Humery. It is sometimes known as the Forty-Two Line Bible, because its Latin text was printed in 42-line columns. Like other publications of that time, Gutenberg's

1517 Italian physician Girolamo Fracastoro proposes that fossils are the petrified remains of once-living organisms.

1518 Smallpox reaches the Americas, carried by European explorers and settlers. The disease decimates native peoples who have no immunity to it.

1517

1518

1518 English physician Thomas Linacre founds the Royal College of Physicians in London.

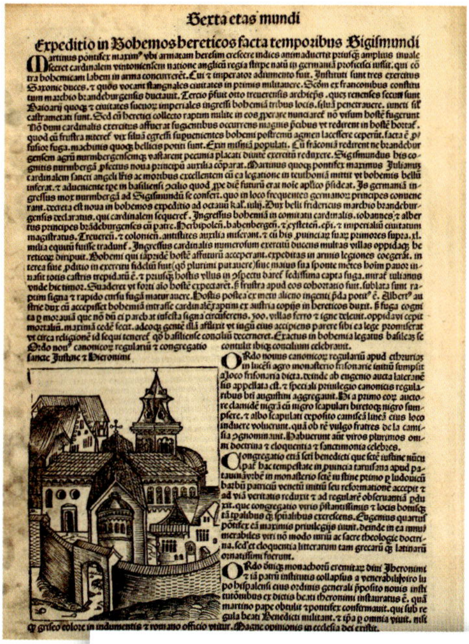
Sexta etas mundi

Expeditio in Bohemos hereticos facta temporibus Sigismundi

The *Nuremberg Chronicle* appeared in 1493, printed from a single plate rather than movable type.

Bible had no page numbers, no title page, and nothing to indicate who had published it. The first printed book in Europe to carry the name of its printer was a book of psalms produced in 1457 by Schöffer. It was also the first book to be printed in two colors. In about 1475, Schöffer, who by then had gone into business on his own, began using steel dies in order to stamp out the copper molds for typecasting.

The Spread of Printing

Printing presses soon began to appear in other parts of Europe. The first press in Italy, at Subiaco near Rome, was established in 1465, and by 1470, the university in Paris, France, had its own press. In 1471, German astronomer and mathematician Regiomontanus (Johannes Müller) set up a press at his Nuremberg observatory for printing astronomical tables, which detailed the movements of the stars and planets.

Metal-type printing was introduced into England by William Caxton (c.1422–c.1491). In 1474, Caxton, working together with the Flemish calligrapher Colard Mansion, had been the first person to print a book in the English language, which he had completed while living in Bruges, Belgium. This book, called the *Recuyell of*

TIMELINE
1519–1525

KEY:

- Astronomy and Math
- Physical and Life Sciences
- Technology

1519 Portuguese navigator Ferdinand Magellan observes the Magellanic clouds, two small galaxies that are the nearest to our own galaxy, the Milky Way.

1519

1519 Swiss-born physician Theophrastus von Hohenheim, better known as Paracelsus, begins writing on medicine. His criticisms of Roman writer Galen helped change medicine.

1520

1520 Returning Spanish voyagers introduce turkeys and corn (maize) from America to Europe.

William Caxton presents one of his books to the English king Edward IV.

The Spread of Printing

Printing with moveable type soon spread across Europe. Printers set up workshops in major cities. There was no copyright law, so many simply printed their own editions of other people's books. Usually, printers did not bind books. The customer bought a collection of loose pages and arranged to have them put into whatever covers they chose. The easy availability of cheaper books helped to spread ideas, such as those of the Protestant Reformation.

Early illustrations were woodcuts, like this 1485 drawing from *The Canterbury Tales.*

the Historyes of Troye, was an account of the Trojan Wars in ancient Greece translated from the original French by Caxton himself. He printed another of his own translations (*The Game and Playe of the Chesse)* a year later. Caxton returned to England in 1476 and set up a printing press in London a year later. In 1481, he published the first illustrated book in English. His Caxton Press published more than 100 works over 15 years. Many books were translations made by Caxton himself, mainly from original French texts.

1522 The expedition of Portuguese sailor Ferdinand Magellan completes the first circumnavigation of the globe (Magellan himself was killed a year earlier).

1522

1522 In China, potters make fine, pale-blue porcelain in the Chia-Ching period.

1525 German mathematician Christoff Rudolf writes the first German book on algebra.

1525

1525 The Swiss-born physician Paracelsus introduces laudanum (tincture of opium) as an anesthetic in medicine.

Leonardo da Vinci

Leonardo was an Italian artist, architect, sculptor, and engineer. He also made many scientific contributions, mainly to anatomy and the design of various mechanisms.

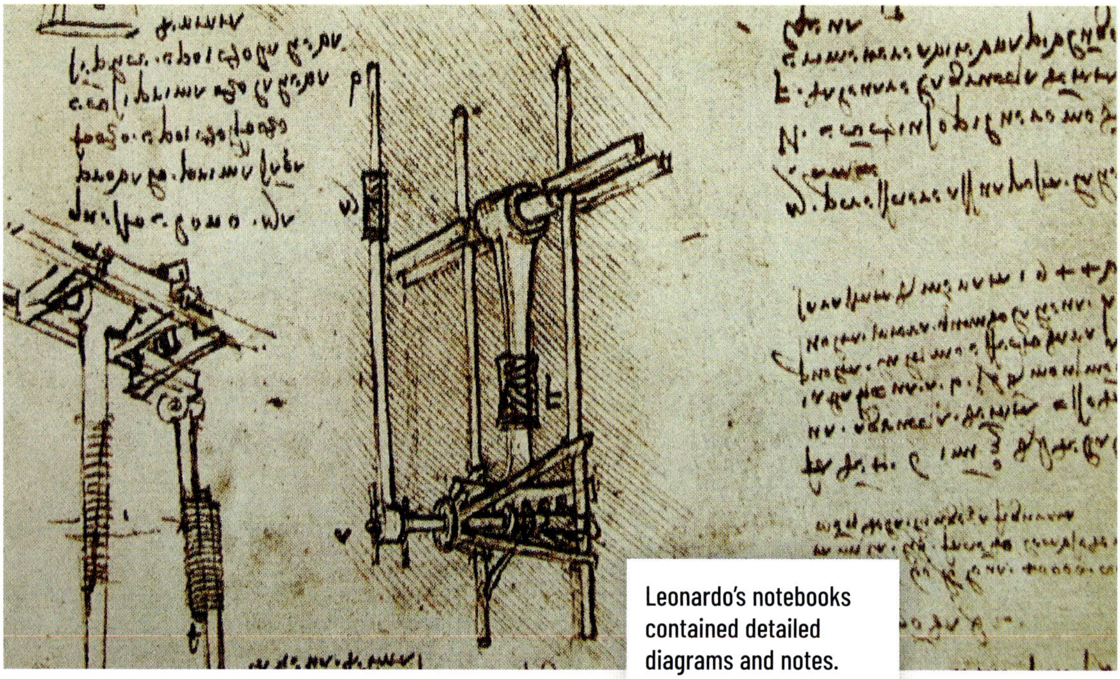

Leonardo's notebooks contained detailed diagrams and notes.

TIMELINE
1525–1533

KEY:

Astronomy and Math

Physical and Life Sciences

Technology

1525 The fusée, a conical pulley that equalizes the pull of a clock's spring as it winds down, is first used in spring-powered clocks.

1526 Spanish explorer Francisco Pizarro enters South America and reaches Peru for the first time.

1527 German astronomer Petrus Apianus includes Pascal's triangle in one of his publications.

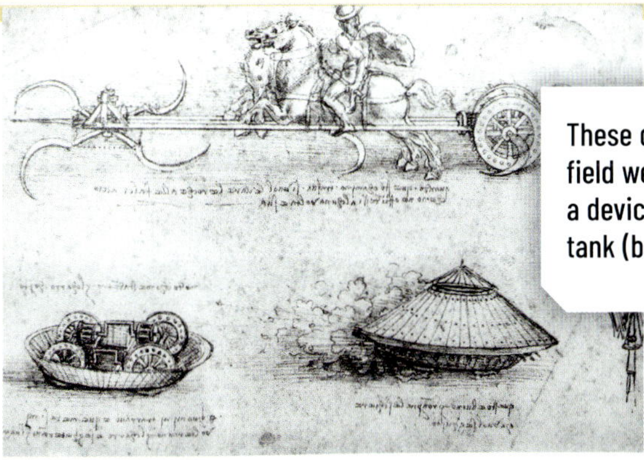

These designs for field weapons show a device similar to a tank (bottom right).

Timeline

1452 Leonardo is born in Vinci

1468 Apprenticed to Verrocchio

1482 Moves to Milan to work for Sforza

1499 Goes to Florence

1502 Works for Cesare Borgia

1506 Returns to Milan to work for Louis XII

1513 Moves to Rome

1516 Goes to Amboise, France

1519 Leonardo da Vinci dies in Amboise

Leonardo was born in Vinci, near Florence in northern Italy, in 1452. At the age of 16, he became an apprentice to artist Andrea del Verrocchio. Leonardo made a series of detailed drawings when preparing sketches for his paintings. Most of our information about Leonardo is from these notebooks.

The Artist's Life

In 1482, Leonardo moved to Milan to work for Ludovico Sforza, later duke of Milan. In 1499, he returned to work in Florence for the soldier, engineer, and architect Cesare Borgia. He painted a series of masterpieces, such as *The Last Supper* and the *Mona Lisa*. After working in Milan again, then for three

Leonardo da Vinci was one of the most versatile men of his time. He left a legacy of paintings, drawings, and notebooks that show an exceptional range of skills.

1530 Italian physician Girolamo Fracastoro observes and describes the disease syphilis among sailors returning from America.

1531 German cartographer Sebastian Münster publishes *Horologiographia*, which describes the construction of sundials.

1530 1531 1533

1530 Swiss cleric Otto Brunfels and German artist Hans Weiditz produce *Living Portraits of Plants*, a book that begins the modern era of descriptive botany.

1533 Dutch mathematician Regnier Gemma Frisius gives the first published account of the use of triangulation in surveying and mapmaking.

Leonardo and Biology

Leonardo wanted to understand how the human body worked, partly so that he could draw it better. He watched dead bodies being dissected and made precise anatomical diagrams of the muscles and the internal organs.

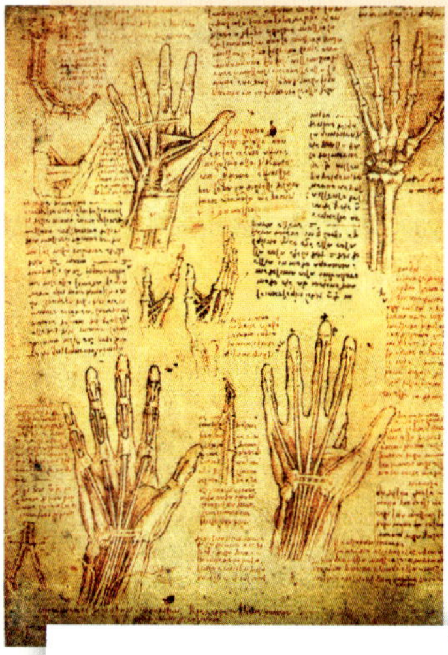

Leonardo made these sketches to learn about the movement of the hands.

years in Rome, Leonardo traveled to Amboise, France, under the patronage of King Francis I (reigned 1515–1547). He was given the title of "first painter, architect, and engineer to the king." Da Vinci remained in France for the rest of his life.

Throughout his long working life, Leonardo made sketches and plans of an amazing range of fortifications, civil engineering schemes, and mechanisms. He described pulleys and belt drives to transmit power, a treadle-operated lathe, a paddle-wheel boat, and a machine for grinding and polishing glass lenses. He invented instruments for measuring the speed of a ship, and for measuring the force of the wind. Starting with a design by Roman architect Marcus Vitruvius Pollio (born c.70 BCE), Leonardo drew up plans for an odometer, a mechanical device to measure the distance traveled by a vehicle. He designed pumps, mechanized vehicles, and even a digging machine for excavating canals. From watching birds in

Leonardo made studies of how tendons and muscles work in the human body.

TIMELINE
1534-1541

KEY:

Astronomy and Math

Physical and Life Sciences

Technology

1534 1535 1536

1534 French navigator Jacques Cartier makes his first voyage to the Gulf of St. Lawrence.

1535 The diving bell comes into use in Europe for working on bridge foundations and shipwrecks underwater.

1536 On his second voyage across the Atlantic, Jacques Cartier claims Canada for France.

flight, he designed an ornithopter, a human-powered, heavier-than-air flying machine with flapping wings. (It could never work because a human could never produce enough power.) There were other impractical designs; a tortoise-shaped tank, a submarine, and a helicopter. His 1485 drawing of a pyramid-shaped parachute was more practical. He is even thought to have made and tested small model parachutes.

Although an exceptional practical engineer, Leonardo did not understand mechanics in any theoretical way (perhaps because he never really learned math), and many of his views on science differed little from the teachings of Greek scientist and philosopher Aristotle (384–322 BCE). Nevertheless, Leonardo's wide-ranging talents spanning the arts and sciences made him the true Renaissance person. When Leonardo died in 1519, his lifelong friend and fellow painter Francesco Melzi (1493–1570) carefully gathered up his paintings, papers, and models made of wood and metal. However, after Melzi's death, many were lost or destroyed. Today, only about 7,000 of the original 13,000 pages of notes have survived, but they are more than enough to testify to Leonardo's genius.

Could Leonardo Fly?

Leonardo drew many flying machines, although no one knows if he ever tried to build any of them. One resembled a helicopter; another was a pyramid-shaped parachute. There were also machines with flapping wings that copied the flight of birds. Most probably would not have worked; they were too heavy or required more power than the human body can produce.

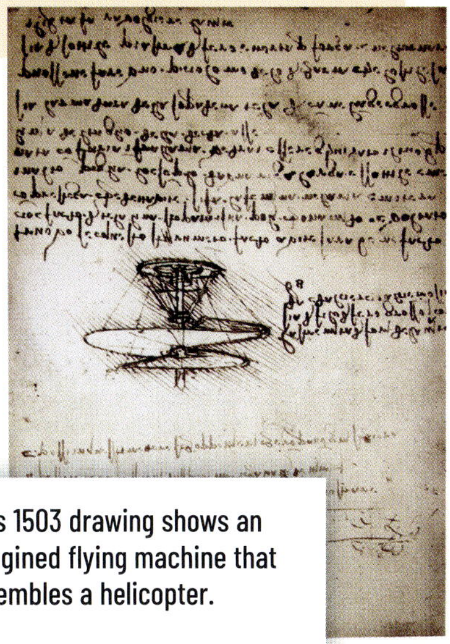

This 1503 drawing shows an imagined flying machine that resembles a helicopter.

1537 Italian mathematician Niccolò Tartaglia invents the gunner's quadrant for aiming cannons.

1540 French surgeon Ambrose Paré makes artificial limbs with joints.

1540 Italian metallurgist Vannoccio Biringuccio describes a pedal-powered machine used for boring cannon barrels.

1541 Austrian astronomer and mathematician Rheticus (Georg Joachim von Lauchen) publishes a set of trigonometrical tables.

Copernicus

"Finally we shall place the Sun himself at the center of the Universe."
(Copernicus: *De Revolutionibus Orbium Coelestium*)

Nicolaus Copernicus spent a lifetime contemplating the heavens.

TIMELINE
1542–1550

KEY:

Astronomy and Math

Physical and Life Sciences

Technology

1542 1543 1544

1542 French physician Jean Fernel explains the condition known as appendicitis.

1543 Polish astronomer Nicolaus Copernicus describes his idea of a sun-centered universe.

1544 German cartographer Sebastian Münster publishes a book on world geography called *Cosmographia Universalis*.

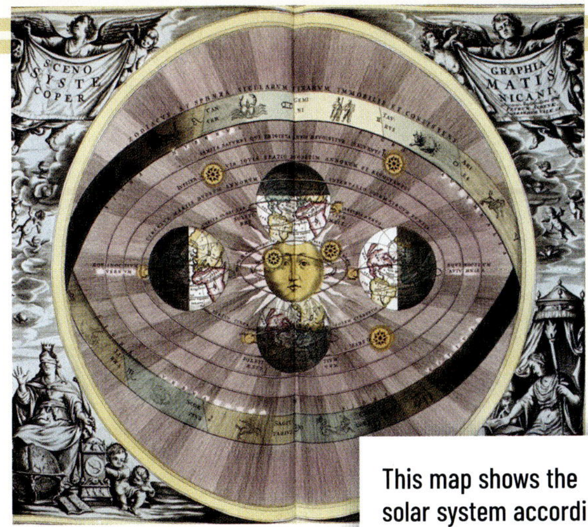

This map shows the solar system according to Copernicus.

Born Mikolaj Kopernik in Poland in 1473, Nicolaus Copernicus changed his name to the familiar version when he was a student. Copernicus' early studies included astronomy, Latin, mathematics, geography, philosophy, Greek, and canon law. The latter led to his appointment as canon of Frauenburg Cathedral in Poland, a position he held for the rest of his life. During the early 1500s, he was granted leave to study medicine at the University of Padua in Italy. But astronomy remained his passion.

The Ptolemaic Universe

Astronomy was still based on the observations of the ancient Greeks Aristotle and Ptolemy and the writings

Timeline

3rd century BCE Aristarchus of Samos proposes the sun-centered universe

1425 Nicholas of Cusa proposes that the sun is at the center of the universe

1473 Copernicus is born in Poland

1506 Copernicus begins work on *De Revolutionibus*

1514 Copernicus publishes his handwritten text *Little Commentary*

1539 Rheticus publishes *Narratio Prima*, previewing Copernicus' work

1543 *De Revolutionibus* is published; Copernicus dies

1545 The French mint introduces a screw press for making coins.

1546 English textile manufacturer William Stumpe sets up a weaving house containing 30 looms and employing 500 people.

1546 Italian physician Girolamo Fracastoro suggests that germs are the cause of disease.

1550 French surgeon Ambrose Paré begins the practice of tying off arteries with ligatures during surgery.

1545 1546 1550

Whose Idea Was It?

Copernicus was not the first person to propose that the planets orbit the sun. The Greek astronomer Aristarchus of Samos suggested the idea in the third century BCE. And in 1425, the German cleric Nicholas of Cusa suggested not only that Earth orbited the sun, but that space was infinite and stars were other suns. Cusa thought there was so much to know that trying to understand it all was like trying to see the corners on a circle.

Copernicus was slow to publish his ideas because he feared the reaction of the Church.

of English mathematician Johannes de Sacrobosco (died c.1256). All assumed that Earth was the center of the universe and that the sun, moon, and planets revolved around it. Ptolemy believed in the perfection of the heavens; he proposed various reasons why the orbits of the celestial bodies were elliptical or oval rather than perfectly circular.

Evolving a Theory

Copernicus realized that many of the problems inherent in Ptolemy's system would disappear if it was accepted that Earth moved around the sun. In 1514, he began distributing copies of a handwritten book, in which he laid out the principles of the heliocentric, or sun-centered, universe, including the suggestion that the apparent rotation of the stars and seasonal movements of the sun are caused by the rotation of Earth on its axis and its movement around the sun. The book became known as the *Little Commentary*. It contained no detailed

TIMELINE
1550–1555

KEY:

Physical and Life Sciences

Technology

1550 Swiss naturalist Konrad von Gesner begins his *Historia Animalium. Animals, Birds,* and *Fish* appear between 1551 and 1558.

1551 English mathematician Leonard Digges invents the theodolite for measuring angles and levels during surveying.

1551 Italian anatomist Gabriello Fallopio discovers the Fallopian tubes linking the ovaries and the womb.

mathematics, and Copernicus did not even put his name to the book. He was saving the details for what he called his "larger work."

Pope Leo X, who commissioned Copernicus to revise the calendar, oversees the burning of books that rejected Church teaching.

Copernicus did not complete this "larger work," the great book *De Revolutionibus Orbium Coelestium* (On the Revolutions of the Heavenly Orbs) until 1530. Being conscious that the Church taught that Earth was the center of God's creation, he allowed the manuscript to be read only by a few scientists.

Stamps from the mid-20th century mark the contribution Copernicus made to astronomy.

Copernicus' student, Rheticus, persuaded him to publish the book and took the manuscript to Nürnberg to be printed. However, the printer was uncomfortable with the implications of a sun-centered universe. He replaced Copernicus' preface to the book with one stating that, in truth, Earth is stationary and that the assumption that it moved around the sun was a device to make the calculations in the book simpler. It seems highly unlikely that Copernicus would have approved of this addition, but he probably never got to read it—by the time the book was published, he was on his deathbed.

1552

1552 Italian anatomist Bartolomeo Eustachio identifies the Eustachian tubes from the middle ear to the throat.

1553

1553 Spanish farmers import European cattle to the pampas of Argentina.

1555

1555 French-born printer Christophe Plantin sets up a print works in Antwerp, Belgium. Some of his type designs are still in use today.

1555 German miners use trucks running on rails, some of which are pushed by hand.

Mercator and Mapmaking

During the 1500s, the science of cartography (mapmaking) advanced greatly. In 1569, Gerardus Mercator devised a way of making maps that is still in use today.

It is difficult to imagine an image of the world without thinking about the shapes of the continents, or the shapes of different countries. But in early maps of the world the now-familiar shapes were drawn very differently. In some maps, the south was at the top of the map—the opposite way to how today's maps are usually drawn.

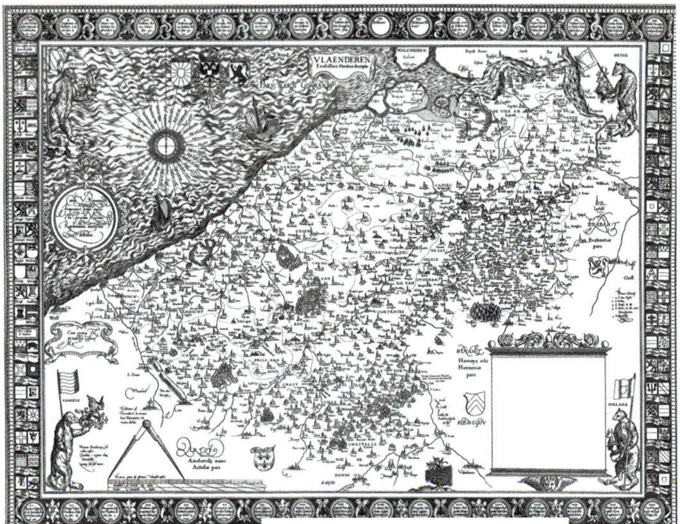

Mercator's map of Flanders, the region of Europe where he was born and made his early studies.

As the European explorers moved across the Atlantic and Indian Oceans in the early 1500s, there was a desire for maps of the world showing the new lands being "discovered." Globes that represented all the known countries and regions of the world were in demand. Gerardus Mercator (1512–1594) was a Flemish

TIMELINE
1556-1563

KEY:

Astronomy and Math

Physical and Life Sciences

Technology

1556 French monk André Thevet introduces tobacco seeds to Europe from Brazil.

1560 Mercury is found in Peru and used in a new process to refine silver.

1556

1560

1556 *De Re Metallica* by German mineralogist Georgius Agricola is published after its author's death. It describes the formation of minerals and has information about mining and metal smelting.

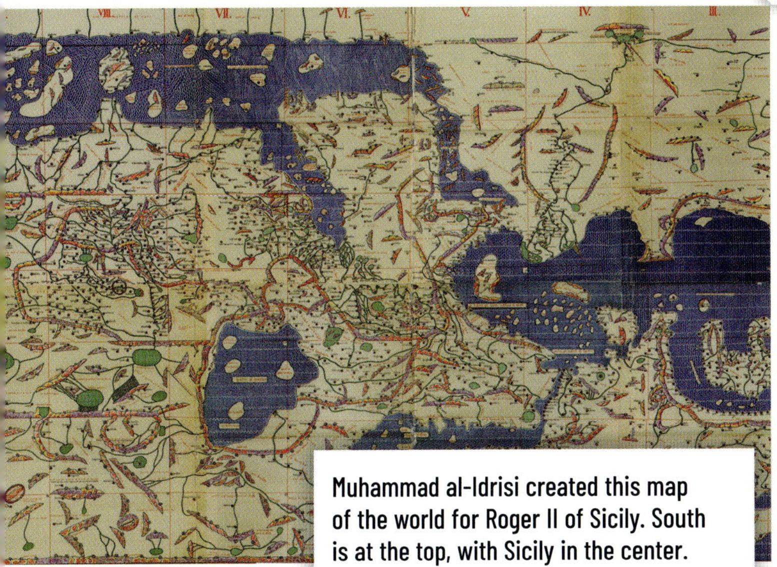

Muhammad al-Idrisi created this map of the world for Roger II of Sicily. South is at the top, with Sicily in the center.

geographer, cosmographer, and cartographer. He was interested in information about the countries of the world and proved skillful at creating globes. In 1541, he produced a terrestrial globe that sold well, and he made a steady living out of this and other globes.

Apart from globes of the whole world, there was also demand for maps that would help sailors to locate where they were in the world. In 1564, Mercator created an accurate map of Great Britain based on information that had been smuggled out of Britain to France by a

Timeline

150 CE Roman geographer Ptolemy produces a world map that includes Europe, China, and India

1154 Muhammad al-Idrisi produces a map of the world for Roger II, King of Sicily

1569 Gerardus Mercator publishes his world map using the Mercator projection

1594 A book of Mercator's maps described as an atlas for the first time

2005 Google Earth uses the Mercator projection, giving smartphone users free access to accurate geographical information

1561 Flemish engineer Pieter Breughel invents a mechanical dredger.

1562 English navigator John Hawkins makes his first visit to the West Indies, mainly to trade slaves from West Africa.

1563 The first potatoes are introduced to England from the Americas.

1561

1562

1563

Mercator produced an accurate map of Great Britain, with west at the top.

Scottish Catholic priest. At the time, religious struggles between Protestants and Catholics in Britain meant that Mercator was aware of the political nature of the map, and the source of his information remained a secret. But there was a problem in creating accurate maps that could be printed on flat pieces of paper—the world is round, not flat. Mercator's solution to this problem was published in 1569 in his world map of that year. He created a map in which the

TIMELINE
1564–1570

KEY:
- Astronomy and Math
- Physical and Life Sciences
- Technology

1564 French physician Ambroise Paré produces his *Treatise on Surgery* describing how patients experience "phantom limb" syndrome after limb amputation.

1567 Italian architect Bartolomeo Ammanati builds the Santa Trinità Bridge, with an elliptical arch, over the Arno River in Florence, Italy.

1567 On a third voyage to the West Indies, John Hawkins is accompanied by the English explorer Francis Drake.

lines of latitude were all parallel to each other and parallel to the equator, as was usual. However, his great breakthrough was that the lines of longitude were also parallel. As can be seen on a globe, the lines of longitude are not parallel in reality. They get closer together as they approach the North and South Poles.

Mercator's Projection

Mercator's map meant that the relative size of countries was not strictly accurate. However, the invaluable advantage for sailors was that it enabled them to set a bearing, called a rhumb line, and then stick to it. The rhumb lines worked as straight lines on the map, accurately reflecting the course the ship was sailing. For this reason, marine charts today are still based on Mercator's projection for navigation.

The map of Europe in Mercator's "Atlas" of 1595, published after his death.

1569 Flemish mapmaker Gerardus Mercator introduces the Mercator map projection for showing the spherical Earth on a flat piece of paper.

1570 Silver from South America reaches China.

1569

1570

1569 Ottoman engineers attempt to construct a canal between the Don and Volga rivers.

1570 Italian architect Andrea Palladio publishes *Four Books on Architecture*, which describes the use of wooden trusses for bridge design.

Galileo Galilei

Galileo, as he is generally known, was a scientist who made fundamental contributions to astronomy, mathematics, and physics.

Galileo made a thermometer from glass vessels holding different liquids floating in a cylinder of water. If the water temperature heats up or cools down, the vessels will rise to the top or sink to the bottom.

TIMELINE

1571–1576

KEY:

- Astronomy and Math
- Physical and Life Sciences
- Technology

1571

1571 Flemish cartographer Abraham Ortelius publishes the first compendium of maps (the word "atlas" is not used until 1594).

1573

1573 Italian anatomist Costanzo Varoli describes the optic nerves.

1573 Danish astronomer Tycho Brahe describes a new supernova in the constellation Cassiopeia.

Galileo gained fame by demonstrating his telescope to Italian high society.

Timeline

1582 Constancy of pendulum's swing

1602 Law of falling bodies

1610 Observes four of Jupiter's moons

1611 First views sunspots

1633 Condemned by the Inquisition

Galileo made major contributions to astronomy, math, and physics.

Galileo was born in Pisa in northern Italy, and educated in Florence and Pisa. He did not get a degree but began working as a teacher. His reputation spread, and in 1589 he became professor of mathematics at Pisa without any formal qualifications. He moved to Padua in 1592 and taught there until 1610.

Observation and Experiment

In 1582, in Pisa Cathedral, Galileo noticed the regular swings of a lamp in a draft. He made his own simple pendulum—like the swinging lamp—with a weight on a length of string, and then

1576 Englishman Robert Norman describes and measures magnetic dip, the downward tilt of a compass needle in Earth's magnetic field.

1573

1576

1573 English sailor Humphrey Cole devises a way to measure a ship's speed by tying a knotted rope to a log, throwing it overboard, and counting how many knots are dragged out in an allotted time.

1576 Danish astronomer Tycho Brahe establishes a purpose-built observatory on the island of Hven in the Baltic Sea.

The Speed of Falling Objects

When Galileo dropped two cannon balls from the Leaning Tower, they fell at the same speed and hit the ground together. He tried to show that they had a constant acceleration (the rate at which speed changes). The diagram shows the results if he could have measured acceleration. As an object falls farther, it moves faster, but the acceleration is constant: 32 feet (9.8 m) per second, which is now known as the acceleration of free fall.

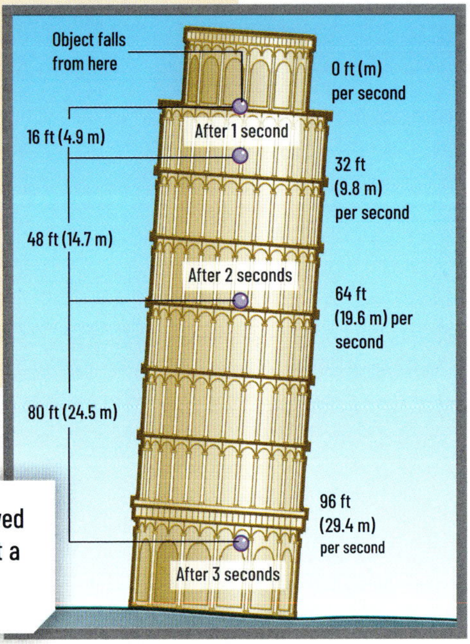

Galileo's experiment showed how objects accelerate at a constant rate.

timed its swings using the beat of his pulse. He found that the time of each swing depended only on the length of the string, not the size of the weight. He suggested that a pendulum could be used to measure time, and pendulums were, in fact, used later to regulate mechanical clocks.

Since the time of the Greeks, people thought that the speed at which an object falls depends on its weight, so a heavier object would fall faster. Galileo put the idea to the test in about 1602. He is said to have dropped two cannonballs of different weights from the Leaning Tower of Pisa and showed that they hit the ground at the same time.

Galileo and Astronomy

The development of the telescope in the early 1600s stimulated Galileo's interest

TIMELINE
1580–1588

KEY:
- Astronomy and Math
- Physical and Life Sciences
- Technology

1580 English explorer Francis Drake completes a full circumnavigation of the globe.

1580 Italian botanist Prospero Alpini makes a distinction between male and female flowers.

1583 Italian botanist and physician Andrea Cesalpino devises a system of classifying plants by their structure.

1584 Italian philosopher and monk Giordano Bruno suggests a theory that the universe is infinite.

in astronomy. He made telescopes of his own and pointed them at the moon. He made drawings recording the moon's mountains and craters at different times during the month. He then studied Jupiter, and in 1610 announced that the planet had four moons of its own. A year later, he aimed his telescope at the sun and noted that sometimes small black spots moved slowly across the sun's disk. The movement of sunspots showed him that the sun is rotating slowly on its axis.

Galileo became convinced that the sun is at the center of the solar system, a theory published in 1543 by Polish astronomer Nicolaus Copernicus. But the idea went against the teachings of Aristotle, who believed in an Earth-centered universe. It was also against the teachings of the Roman Catholic Church. Church officials asked Galileo not to spread the idea, but in 1632 he published it in a book, which was banned. In 1633, he was arrested by the Inquisition, taken to Rome, and under threat of torture, made to recant his views.

Under House Arrest

Old and in failing health, Galileo was banished to his home near Florence. He went blind in 1637, possibly from damage caused by looking at the sun. Galileo's failing eyesight made him bitter because he could no longer observe the universe. When he died in 1642, he was suffering from arthritis and high blood pressure. Pope Urban VIII refused to forget his feud with Galileo, and Galileo was buried with no ceremony in the Church of Santa Croce in Florence.

DIALOGO
DI
GALILEO GALILEI LINCEO
MATEMATICO SOPRAORDINARIO
DELLO STVDIO DI PISA.
E Filosofo, e Matematico primario del
SERENISSIMO
GR.DVCA DI TOSCANA.
Doue ne i congressi di quattro giornate si discorre sopra i due
MASSIMI SISTEMI DEL MONDO TOLEMAICO, E COPERNICANO;
Proponendo indeterminatamente le ragioni Filosofiche, e Naturali tanto per l'vna, quanto per l'altra parte.
CON PRI VILEGI.
IN FIORENZA, Per Gio:Batista Landini MDCXXXII.
CON LICENZA DE' SVPERIORI.

Galileo's 1632 book about the universe was banned by the Catholic Church.

1588 English cleric Timothy Bright invents a system of shorthand writing that uses symbols to denote words.

1585

1588

1585 Flemish mathematician and engineer Simon Stevin, known as Stevinus, introduces decimal fractions into common use.

1588 English cleric William Lee invents a stocking frame, a knitting machine for making hosiery.

William Harvey

William Harvey changed the way that physicians thought about the circulation of the blood after he had carried out many detailed experiments.

From ancient times, no one had any doubt about the importance of the blood in animals, particularly in humans. Bleeding was a sign that something was wrong, and could lead to death if it was not stopped. The problem for physicians was to understand why blood in the veins was different from the much brighter blood in the arteries.

The influential Roman doctor Galen, writing in about 150 CE, had put forward the theory that there were two different networks through which blood flowed in the body. Blood in the veins was centred on the liver, but the blood in arteries was pumped through the body by the heart. These different types of blood were created by the liver or the heart, and then used by the body. Medieval researchers saw that blood came into the heart from the veins, but they were not able to work out why blood

William Harvey made a profound improvement in medicine by showing there was a single circulatory system.

TIMELINE
1590–1597

KEY:

Astronomy and Math

Physical and Life Sciences

Technology

1590 Italian architects Giacomo della Porta and Domenico Fontana complete the vaulting of the dome on St. Peter's Basilica in Rome, designed by Michelangelo.

1590

1590 Dutch optician Zacharias Jansen invents the compound microscope, which has two lenses, one for the eyepiece and one for the objective lens.

An 18th-century drawing of Galen, the Roman doctor whose views on blood circulation were proved wrong by Harvey.

came out of the heart as brighter, arterial blood.

Observation

During the 1500s, various physicians tried to solve this puzzle. All were unsuccessful until William Harvey (1578–1657) began his experiments in the early 1600s. Harvey was a well-traveled and well-connected man. He graduated as a physician from the University of Padua in Italy in 1602, and by 1618 had been appointed physician to King James I of England and Scotland. He was firmly against superstition, and believed that accusations of witchcraft against women, common at the time, were wrong.

Timeline

1600 BCE Egyptian doctors recognize that blood takes air from the lungs around the body

150 CE Galen describes the heart and liver as creating blood in two different systems

1242 Muslim researcher Ibn al-Nafis describes how blood goes from the heart to the lungs, mixes with air, and is sent into the body via the pulmonary artery

1628 Harvey's *Exercitatio Anatomica de Motu Cordis et Sanguinis in Animalibus* published

1661 Capillaries identified by Malpighi using a microscope; shows that Harvey's view of one circulatory system had been correct

1592 Italian scientist Galileo Galilei makes an air-filled, open-ended, liquid-in-glass thermometer.

1594 Scottish mathematician John Napier devises "natural" logarithms, which he publishes in table form in 1614.

1596 English writer John Harrington invents a flushing toilet, the water closet (WC).

1597 Italian surgeon Gaspare Tagliacozzi practices rhinoplasty (surgery to reshape the nose).

1592 1594 1596 1597

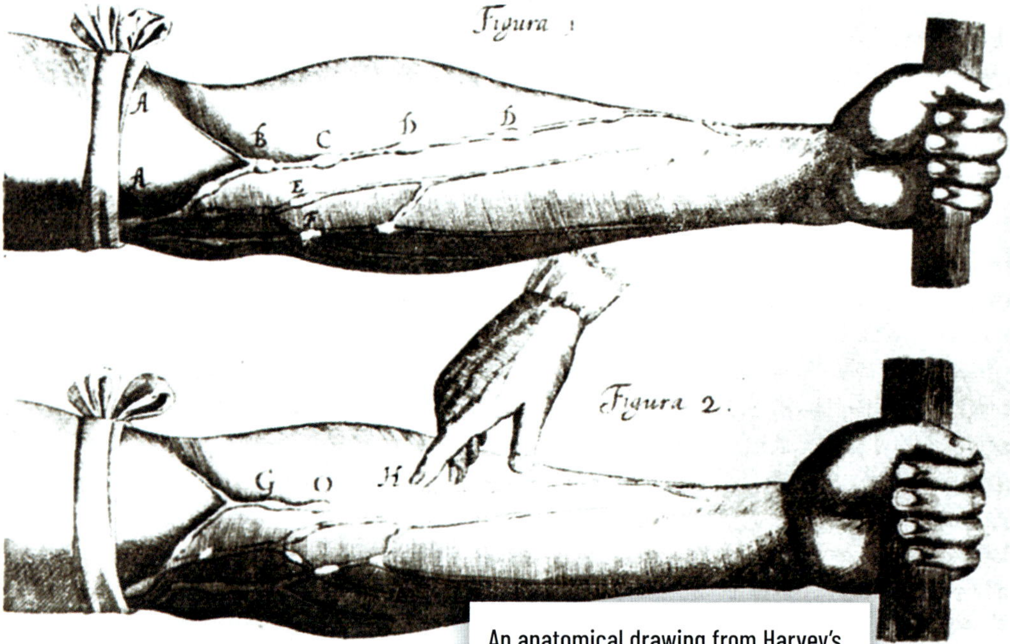

An anatomical drawing from Harvey's 1628 work on blood circulation.

Harvey made many experiments on cold-blooded creatures, such as frogs, where the blood flow was easier to understand. He carefully recorded his results. In his major work *Exercitatio Anatomica de Motu Cordis et Sanguinis in Animalibus (An Anatomical Exercise on the Motion of the Heart and Blood in Living Beings)* of 1628, Harvey first described how the left ventricle and right ventricle of the heart

TIMELINE
1597–1604

KEY:

- Astronomy and Math
- Physical and Life Sciences
- Technology

1597 German chemist Andreas Libau prepares hydrochloric acid.

1598 Dutch inventor Cornelis van Drebbel patents the first "self-winding" clock.

1599 Flemish engineer and mathematician Stevinus builds a "land yacht," a wind-powered carriage with sails.

1597 1598 1599

moved together, and not independently. He showed clearly that Galen's theory that blood was created in the heart and the liver could not be correct. Harvey went on to demonstrate that the veins are part of the same system as the arteries. The circulatory system was a single unit, in which blood flow was controlled by the contraction and expansion of muscles in the heart.

Harvey Proved Right

Harvey's theory attracted much criticism. This was partly because he opposed Galen, who was thought of as the greatest medical thinker at the time. Neither could Harvey show how the veins and arteries were linked. He thought that blood was absorbed into tissue from arteries and then reabsorbed into veins to take it back to the heart. Only when the microscope was invented decades later were the tiny capillaries that link arteries with veins identified.

Marcello Malpighi's use of a microscope enabled him to see capillaries linking arteries with veins, so proving Harvey's theory of blood circulation correct.

1600 English physician William Gilbert describes the magnetic properties of Earth.

1602 Italian scientist Galileo Galilei formulates the law of falling bodies; they fall with equal speed regardless of their weight.

1603 Italian anatomist Hieronymus Fabricius d'Aquapendente gives the first clear description of the valves in veins.

1604 German astronomer Johannes Kepler discovers a supernova in the constellation Ophiuchus; it becomes known as Kepler's star.

The Pendulum Clock

Metal clocks powered by falling weights date from the 1300s, but they were inaccurate. A way to regulate the mechanism was needed, and that arrived in the 1600s.

The pendulum clock depends on the gradual release of energy from the clock's main spring.

TIMELINE
1605–1610

KEY:

- Astronomy and Math
- Physical and Life Sciences
- Technology

1605 1606 1608

1605 German astronomer Christoph Scheiner invents the pantograph, a device for tracing drawings in order to reduce or enlarge them.

1606 German chemist Andreas Libau writes *Alchymia*, the first modern chemistry textbook.

1608 German-born Dutch lensmaker Hans Lippershey makes a refracting telescope (using two lenses).

In 1582, the Italian scientist Galileo Galilei showed that a pendulum always swings at a constant rate. He also proved that the rate of swing depends on the length of the pendulum, not on the size of its weight. The time taken for one swing is proportional to the square root of the length of the pendulum. A pendulum 39 inches (99 cm) long takes one second to make one swing (forward and back). If it keeps swinging, it can mark off time.

Galileo instructed his son Vincenzo how to make a clock regulated by a pendulum. Vincenzo did not complete the job, and it was not until 1657 that the first pendulum clock appeared. It was designed by the Dutch scientist Christiaan Huygens and kept time to within five minutes a day, far more accurate than earlier clocks.

Timeline

1641 Galileo's pendulum clock design

1656 Huygens' pendulum clock

1726 Graham's mercury pendulum

1728 Harrison's gridiron pendulum

Christiaan Huygens is credited with inventing a practical pendulum clock.

Importance of Temperature

Clock pendulums use a metal rod. However, the length of the rod does not stay the same length. It varies depending on temperature. The rod gets longer when it is warm and shorter when it is cold. A clock with a one-second pendulum, for

1609 Johannes Kepler draws up his first two laws of planetary motion.

1610 French astronomer Nicolas-Claude Fabri de Peiresc discovers the Orion Nebula.

1609

1610

1609 Dutch inventor Cornelis van Drebbel invents an incubator for hens' eggs.

1610 Italian scientist Galileo Galilei uses the newly invented telescope to observe four of Jupiter's moons and sees craters on the moon.

The Anchor Escapement

In a mechanical clock, the rate at which power "escapes" from the weight is controlled by a mechanism known as an escapement. An anchor escapement on the pendulum gives a rocking motion to the anchor. It stops and starts the escape wheel, letting it gradually release the power of the falling weight that then provides the force that drives the main wheel.

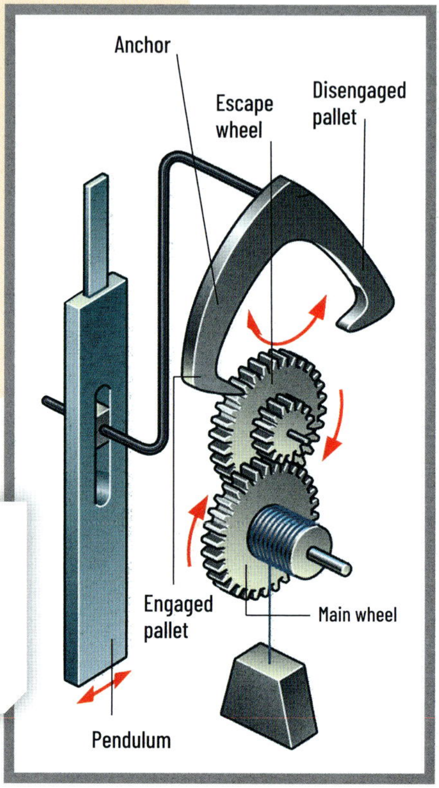

With an anchor escapement, the hour hand of the clock is attached to the axle of the main wheel.

instance, needs an increase of just 0.0009 inch (0.023 mm) in order to lose about one second a day. A steel rod expands by that much with a rise in temperature of only 4°F (2°C). The reason that a grandfather clock is so tall is that it has to be long enough to house a 39-inch (99-cm) one-second pendulum, common to all such clocks. They go "tick, tock" every second.

Inventors devised ways of making a pendulum of constant length. English inventor George Graham designed the mercury pendulum (announced in 1726), which has a glass jar of mercury as the pendulum's weight. When the pendulum expands because of a rise in temperature, the change is balanced by the upward expansion of the mercury in the jar.

TIMELINE
1611–1619

KEY:

Astronomy and Math

Physical and Life Sciences

Technology

1611 German astronomer Christoph Scheiner observes sunspots (independently of Galileo).

1612 German astronomer and mathematician Simon Marius publishes the first description of the Andromeda Galaxy.

Galileo used his own pulse to time the swinging of a lamp in Pisa Cathedral.

The Constant Pendulum

Galileo noticed that a pendulum has a constant rate of swing. That rate depends on the pendulum's length, not its weight. In mathematical terms, the time of the swing (its period) is proportional to the square root of the length of the pendulum. A longer period needs a longer pendulum.

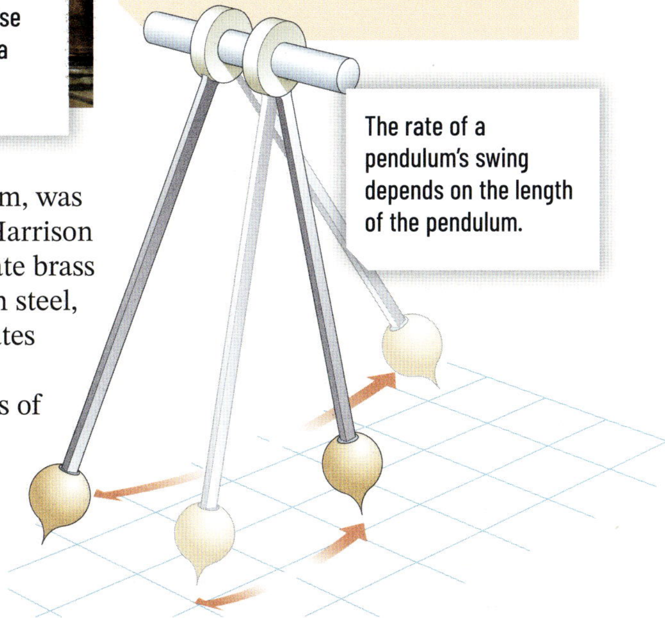

The rate of a pendulum's swing depends on the length of the pendulum.

Another solution, the gridiron pendulum, was invented by English clockmaker John Harrison in 1728. His design has a grid of alternate brass and steel rods. Brass expands more than steel, so the expansion of the brass compensates for the lesser expansion of steel. A pendulum rod made of concentric tubes of iron and zinc achieves a similar result. Today, pendulum rods are made from invar, an alloy of iron and nickel that expands very little when heated.

1614 1617 1618 1619

1614 Italian physician Sanctorius begins the study of the body's metabolism.

1617 Scottish mathematician John Napier introduces "Napier's bones," strips of bone or wood that use logarithms to aid calculations.

1618 William Oughtred, an English mathematician, introduces the letter "x" in math as the multiplication sign.

1619 English ironmaster Dud Dudley claims to smelt iron using "pit coal" (rather than charcoal). He patents the process two years later.

The Barometer and Vacuums

In the 1640s, an Italian set out to measure air pressure, caused by the weight of the atmosphere. He proved the existence of the vacuum and invented the barometer.

The Magdeburg spheres, invented by Otto von Guericke, were copper hemispheres. After the air had been pumped out, creating a vacuum, 16 horses could not pull them apart.

TIMELINE
1620–1624

KEY:

Astronomy and Math

Physical and Life Sciences

Technology

1620 English mathematician Edmund Gunter introduces the 22-yard (20-m) surveyor's chain, which becomes a standard unit of measurement.

1620

1620 English philosopher Francis Bacon advocates a scientific method of testing a theory by a controlled experiment (hypothesis, experiment, conclusion).

In 1645, Evangelista Torricelli (1608–1647), a mathematician and former assistant to Galileo, took a 6.6-foot (2-m) glass tube, sealed at one end, and filled it with mercury. Keeping his thumb over the open end, he upended the tube in a dish full of mercury and then removed his thumb. Some mercury ran out into the dish, and the mercury level in the tube dropped to about 30 inches (76 cm). He wondered what was stopping it all from escaping.

Atmospheric Pressure

Torricelli reasoned that the weight of the atmosphere (air) pressing on the surface of the mercury in the dish equaled the weight of the mercury left in the tube. The height of the mercury column is therefore a measure of air pressure. The whole device is known as a barometer. Torricelli also noticed that the height of the column varied depending on the weather and thought that atmospheric pressure must also vary. In 1647, French mathematician René Descartes added a vertical scale to a Torricelli barometer and

Timeline

1645 Mercury barometer

1654 Magdeburg spheres

1703 Hawksbee's vacuum pump

1771 Barometer as altimeter

1855 Geissler's vacuum pump

1865 Sprengel's mercury vapor pump

Von Guericke uses weights to test the strength of a vacuum inside a sphere.

1622 English mathematician William Oughtred creates the slide rule, which uses logarithms to perform multiplication and division.

1623 In *Pinax Theatri Botanici,* Swiss botanist Gaspard Bauhin describes 6,000 different plants.

1624 Flemish physician and chemist Jan Baptista van Helmont invents the word "gas."

1624 English mathematician Henry Briggs publishes tables to "common" logarithms from 1 to 100,000.

Torricelli created the first vacuum. This led to the invention of the barometer and showed that vacuums exist.

used it to record weather observations. Pressure is still sometimes measured in inches or millimeters of mercury—"normal" pressure is 30 inches (760 mm). Atmospheric pressure also varies with altitude. The pressure at the top of a mountain is less than that at the foot of the mountain. In 1771, Swiss geologist Jean Deluc began using a sensitive barometer to measure the heights of mountains. A modern altimeter, used in airplanes, is also a modified barometer. Torricelli's barometer was not easy to move around, even if Jean Deluc carried one up mountains. In 1797, a French scientist, Jean Nicolas Fortin (1750–1831), invented a portable mercury barometer.

In Torricelli's original experiment, what was in the space above the mercury in the closed tube? It was a vacuum, a space in which there is nothing at all.

Understanding Vacuums

Scientists studying vacuums needed a way to produce them in the laboratory. In 1654, Otto von Guericke, mayor of Magdeburg, Germany, invented the first air pump, so-called because it was designed to pump air out of a vessel. (Today we would call it a vacuum pump.) He used it to remove the air from between a pair of copper hemispheres, which became held tightly together by the force of atmospheric pressure. Even 16 horses could not pull them apart. Von Guericke's apparatus became known as the Magdeburg spheres, although they were hemispheres.

More efficient pumps followed. In 1703, English physicist

TIMELINE
1625–1629

KEY:

- Astronomy and Math
- Physical and Life Sciences
- Technology

1625 English physician John Woodall becomes examiner of the Barber-Surgeon Company. He recommends using lemons to counter scurvy in sailors.

1626 St. Peter's Basilica in Rome is finally consecrated, having taken 120 years to build.

1627 German astronomer Johannes Kepler publishes the *Rudolphine Tables*, describing the motions of the planets.

Torricelli's mercury tube barometer can be replicated today with simple equipment.

The Mercury Barometer

To recreate Torricelli's original experiment, a closed glass tube is filled with mercury and placed upside down in a dish of mercury. The mercury level in the tube falls slightly, leaving a vacuum in the space above. Atmospheric pressure acting on the mercury in the dish holds up the mercury column. The height of the column above the surface of the dish measures the atmospheric pressure.

Francis Hawksbee made a vacuum pump that Irish scientist Robert Boyle used to study gases. German physicist Heinrich Geissler used his pump of 1855 to study electrical discharges at low pressures, and 10 years later, German-born British scientist Hermann Sprengel mechanized Geissler's pump. Still used today, it is a mercury vapor pump (or diffusion pump) in which the vapor "captures" molecules of air and carries them away to produce a vacuum. It had some important applications, leading to the discovery of the electron, the finding of rare gases in air, and the invention of the electric lightbulb.

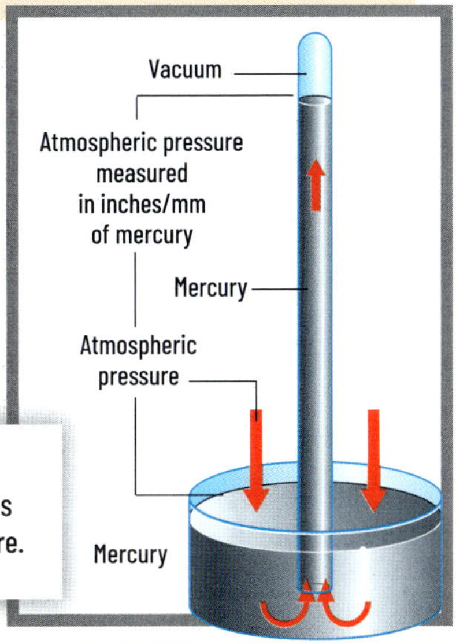

The barometer proves and measures atmospheric pressure.

1629 Italian engineer Giovanni Branca makes a primitive steam turbine.

1628 1629

1628 English physician William Harvey explains the circulation of the blood—the way in which the heart pumps blood through the lungs and around the body.

Isaac Newton

Isaac Newton made fundamental breakthroughs in mathematics and established the basic laws that became the cornerstones of astronomy and physics.

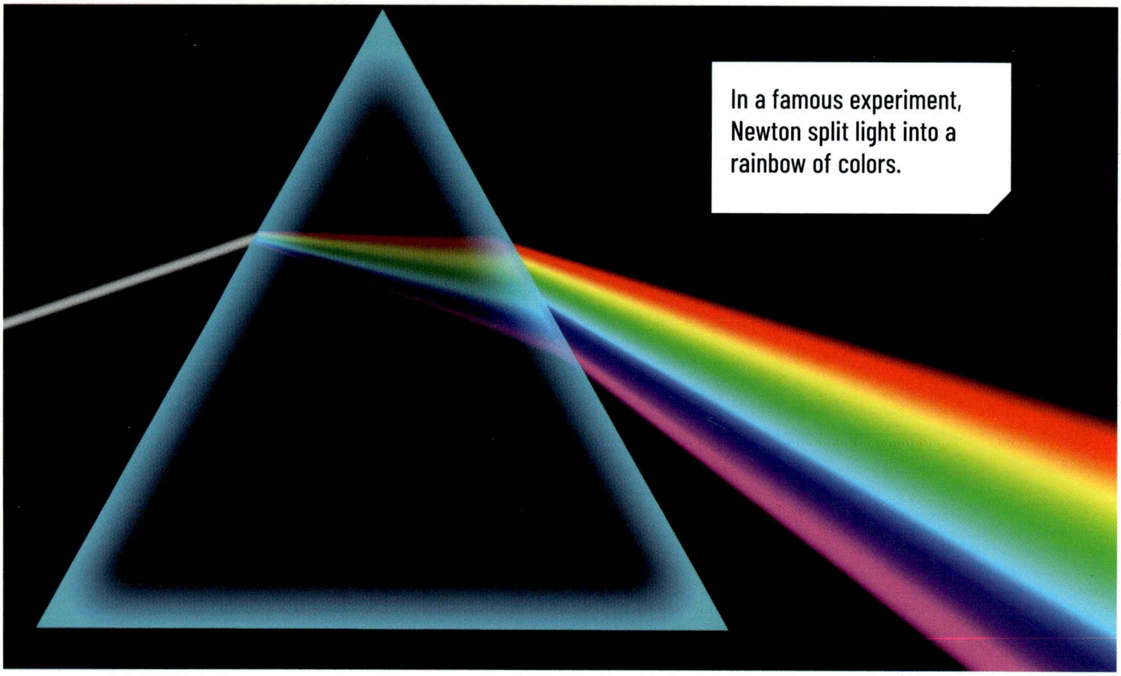

In a famous experiment, Newton split light into a rainbow of colors.

TIMELINE
1630–1638

KEY:

Astronomy and Math

Physical and Life Sciences

1630 Jesuit priests bring the bark of the South American cinchona tree to Europe to treat malaria; it is later found to contain the drug quinine.

1631 English mathematician Thomas Harriot introduces the symbols < and >, meaning "less than" and "more than," respectively.

1631 French astronomer Pierre Gassendi makes the first observation of the transit of the planet Mercury across the sun.

Newton was born in a rural home and spent most of his life outside London.

Isaac Newton was born in Lincolnshire, a rural area of eastern England. He was brought up by his grandmother and educated at a local school before going to Trinity College (Cambridge University). He received his bachelor's degree from Cambridge in 1665, but was forced to remain in the country town rather than heading into London, as many promising academics did, because of the plague that was raging in the capital at that time. At first, Newton's graduate studies concentrated on mathematics, working out the principles of "fluxions," which were to lead to the development of differential calculus.

Timeline

1642 Newton born in Lincolnshire, England

1665 Binomial theorem (math)

c.1665 Law of gravity and center of gravity

1668 Newton's reflecting telescope

1671 Splits white light into a spectrum

1675 Corpuscular theory of light

1678 Robert Hooke's law of gravity

1687 Book *Principia* published

1703 Newton elected president of the Royal Society

1704 Book *Opticks* published

1705 Newton is knighted

1727 Dies in London

1632 The first modern observatory is built at Leyden (now Leiden) in the Netherlands.

1633 Italian scientist Galileo Galilei is sentenced to house arrest by the Inquisition for refusing to withdraw his claim that the sun, not Earth, is the center of the universe.

1637 French mathematician René Descartes introduces analytic geometry, a way to use algebraic equations to represent geometric lines and curves.

1638 English astronomer William Gascoigne and Frenchman Adrien Auzout independently invent the eyepiece micrometer, which enables accurate measurements to be made using telescopes and microscopes.

Newton studied at Trinity College, Cambridge, and became a professor there.

Laws of Motion

In 1667, Newton received a fellowship from Trinity College. In 1699, he became a professor of mathematics at Trinity and turned his attention to what happens when objects move—what makes them start moving and what stops them. His conclusions are summed up in Newton's three laws of motion (see page 44). All of these laws can be observed by watching a game of pool.

Law of Gravitation

Newton's next contribution was to have a profound effect on astronomy. According to the well-known story—which likely never happened—he was sitting in an orchard when he saw an apple fall. (In some versions of the story, the apple fell on his head.) Why did the apple fall? Whatever prompted his investigations, Newton concluded that the apple must be attracted to Earth by a force, which we now call gravity. He also deduced that every object behaves as if its mass were

TIMELINE

1639–1642

KEY:

- Astronomy and Math
- Physical and Life Sciences
- Technology

1639 English astronomers William Crabtree and Jeremiah Horrocks make the first observation of the transit of Venus across the sun.

1639 A glassworks set up in Plymouth, Maryland, is one of the first "factories" in Britain's American colonies.

1640 French mathematician Pierre de Fermat proposes Fermat's principle: light always travels in a straight line.

concentrated in one place, its center of gravity (now called the center of mass). Applying his own laws of motion, he figured out that all objects in the universe are affected by such gravitational forces—it is gravity that keeps the moon in orbit around Earth and Earth in orbit around the sun. He produced a formula, the universal law of gravitation, that states the gravitational force between any two objects—whether they are two pool balls or two stars—is equal to the product of their masses and inversely proportional to the distance between them. The English scientist Robert Hooke also devised a law of gravity in about 1678 and published his ideas a few years later. This led to a bitter dispute between the two great men.

Newton's Law of Gravity

Isaac Newton formulated his law of gravity to deal with the attractive force (gravitation) that exists between any two objects that have mass. The strength of the force depends on how close the two objects are (the nearer they are, the stronger is the force trying to pull them together) and how massive they are (the more massive they are, the stronger the force between them—we don't notice the pull of smaller objects). In mathematical terms, the gravitational force is proportional to the product of the masses and inversely proportional to the distance between them.

Newton's laws explained the force of gravity in terms of distance and mass.

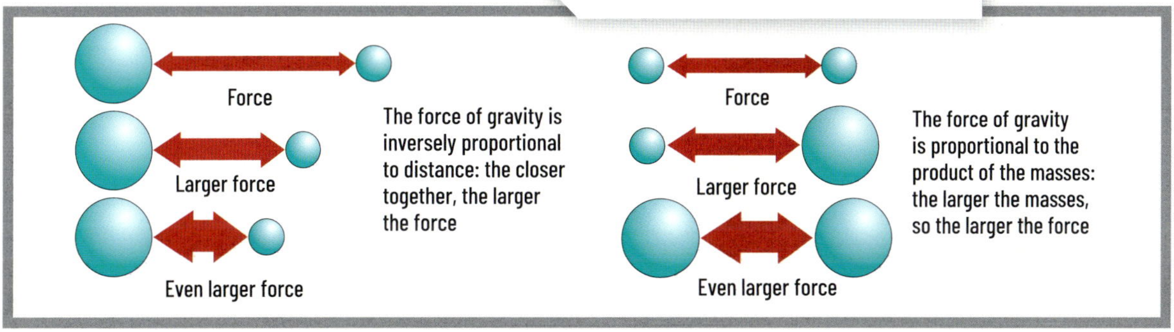

1641 Dutch naturalist Nicolaas Tulp describes a chimpanzee brought to the Netherlands; the chimpanzee was the first of the great apes to be discovered.

1642 Pascal proposes Pascal's law, which states that the pressure within a liquid is the same everywhere. The principle underlies all hydraulic machinery.

1641

1642

1642 French scientist Blaise Pascal builds a wooden mechanical calculating machine—it is an early step toward a computer.

1642 German anatomist Johann Wirsung discovers the pancreatic duct, which carries digestive juices to the duodenum.

Newton's Laws of Motion

In addition to his law of gravity, Newton also formulated laws about another major area of physics: motion. Newton's first law of motion states that an object at rest will remain at rest (and a moving object will continue moving) unless an outside force acts on it. According to Newton's second law, force can be defined as something that makes an object accelerate (force equals mass times acceleration). The third law states that for every "action" (a force that one object exerts on another) there is an equal and opposite "reaction" (exerted by the second object on the first).

All three of Newton's laws of motion can be seen during a game of pool.

Optical Studies

In the branch of physics we now call optics, Newton's main studies concerned the nature of light. By allowing a narrow beam of white light from the sun to pass through a glass prism—where the angles caused the light to refract, or bend—Newton split the light into a multicolored spectrum, the sequence of colors seen in a rainbow. He showed that white light is actually made up of a variety of colors. (Today, we say that it is made of many different wavelengths.)

Telescopes of the time often produced images that were surrounded by a spectrum of colors because the poor-quality lenses brought different colors into focus in different places. Newton overcame the problem by using mirrors instead of lenses to focus the image. In 1668, he produced one of the first reflecting telescopes with mirrors he made himself.

TIMELINE
1645–1650

KEY:

- Astronomy and Math
- Physical and Life Sciences
- Technology

1645 English physician Daniel Whistler first diagnoses the childhood disease rickets.

1645 Italian physicist Evangelista Torricelli constructs the first mercury barometer.

1646 The English scientist Thomas Browne coins the word "electricity" (which at the time referred only to static electricity).

This diagram from Newton's book *Opticks* of 1704 shows a prism splitting a ray of white light into a spectrum.

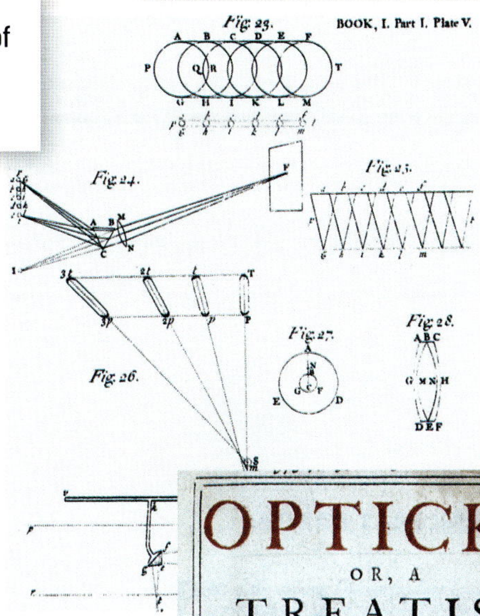

Newton was convinced that light is composed of a "flux" of minute particles ("corpuscles"). However, his theory was soon challenged by Christiaan Huygens and others, who suggested that light instead travels as waves. The argument raged on between scientists until the 20th century, when physicists finally concluded that light has properties of both particles and waves; but this realization had to await the development of quantum theory.

In 1703, Newton was elected president of the Royal Society, and two years later he was knighted (the first scientist to receive the honor). As Sir Isaac Newton, he continued to be showered with honors. His final tribute was a state funeral and burial in Westminster Abbey, London. His name lives on in the SI unit of force, which is called the newton (the force that gives 1 kilogram an acceleration of 1 meter per second per second, or 1 meter per second squared).

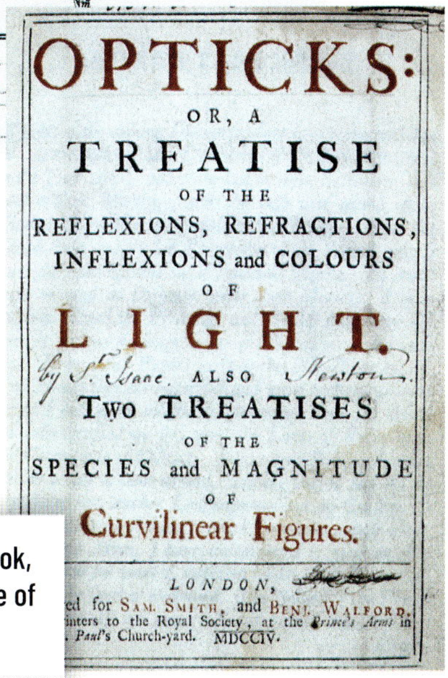
OPTICKS:
OR, A
TREATISE
OF THE
REFLEXIONS, REFRACTIONS, INFLEXIONS and COLOURS
OF
LIGHT.
ALSO
Two TREATISES
OF THE
SPECIES and MAGNITUDE
OF
Curvilinear Figures.
LONDON,
...ed for SAM. SMITH, and BENJ. WALFORD, ...inters to the Royal Society, at the Prince's Arms in ... Paul's Church-yard. MDCCIV.

The title page of Newton's 1704 book, which created the modern science of optics, or the study of light.

1647 French scientist Blaise Pascal builds a primitive version of the roulette wheel to test his ideas on probability.

1649 English physician Henry Power discovers the extremely narrow capillary blood vessels.

1650 German scholar Athanasius Kircher demonstrates that sound does not travel in a vacuum.

1650 German inventor Stephen Farfler constructs a three-wheeled chair, an early wheelchair.

1647 1649 1650

Telescopes

The first lenses were used mainly as magnifying glasses. But scientists and astronomers wanted to see distant objects. The telescope made this possible.

Isaac Newton built his reflecting telescope in 1668; it magnified objects about 40 times.

TIMELINE
1650–1657

KEY:

- Astronomy and Math
- Physical and Life Sciences
- Technology

1650 The first properly equipped chemistry laboratory is established at the University of Leyden (now Leiden) in the Netherlands.

1652 Dutch hydraulic engineer Cornelius Vermuyden drains the Fens, a large marsh region in eastern England.

1653 French scientist Blaise Pascal devises Pascal's triangle, in which each number is the sum of the two numbers above it.

Hans Lippershey, the German-born Dutch eyeglass maker, made his first telescope in 1608. He sold his invention to the Dutch government for use by the military. News of the device reached the Italian scientist Galileo Galilei, who immediately made his own telescopes to study the heavens. Among his discoveries were sunspots, craters on the moon, and the four major moons of Jupiter.

Improving the View

In 1611, German Christoph Scheiner made a telescope that provided a wider field of view by using two convex lenses. Called an astronomical telescope, it produces an upside-down image. For centuries afterward, images of the moon, for instance, were always shown with "north" at the bottom.

Lenses of the time suffered from defects such as chromatic aberration, in which a fringe of color surrounded an image. They could be improved by grinding and polishing lenses. But it was not until 1758 that Englishman John Dollond made an achromatic telescope. His

Timeline

1608 First refracting telescope

1655 Huygens' improved refractor

1663 Gregory's reflecting telescope

1668 Newton's reflecting telescope

1672 Cassegrain's improved reflector

1758 Dollond's achromatic telescope

This monument at the Griffith Park Observatory in Los Angeles shows astronomical pioneers Johannes Kepler, Galileo Galilei, and Nicolaus Copernicus.

1654 1655 1656 1657

1654 German physicist Otto von Guericke invents an air pump (vacuum pump).

1655 Dutch scientist Christiaan Huygens uses a homemade telescope to observe the rings around the planet Saturn.

1656 Huygens invents a pendulum clock.

1657 Huygens writes the first book on mathematical probability theory.

Refracting and Reflecting Telescopes

One kind of refracting telescope is the type originally designed by Galileo in 1609 (below left). It uses two lenses and produces an upright image. Small versions can be paired to form binoculars. Of the two reflecting designs also shown below, the Newtonian has the eyepiece at the side, which can be inconvenient in a large telescope. The Cassegrainian telescope has the eyepiece at the lower end, where it is easier to use.

method, still used today, involves making a compound lens with two components stuck together. The second component, made of crown glass, corrects the aberrations caused by the first component, which is made out of flint glass. It works because the two types of glass bend light rays in slightly different ways.

Another method of avoiding chromatic aberration involved using lenses with slight curvature and therefore a long focal length (the distance from the main mirror or object lens to the eyepiece). This meant making telescopes very long. Telescopes measuring 33 feet (10 m) long were common.

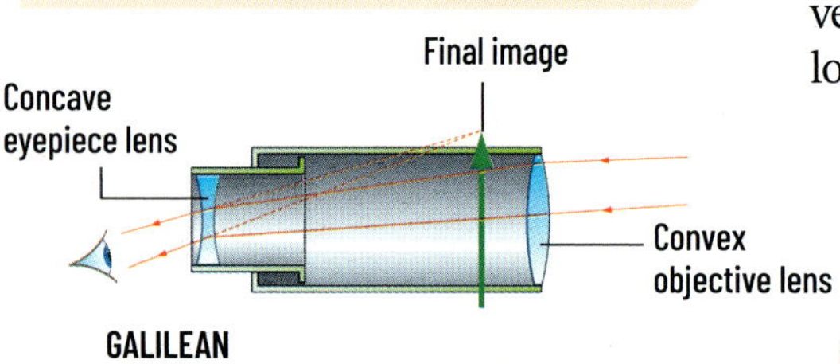

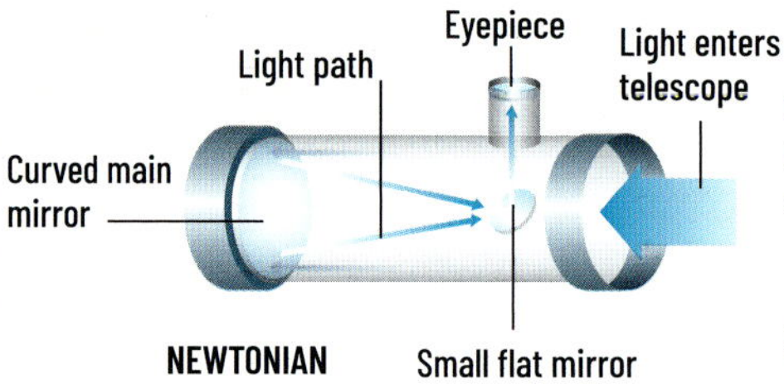

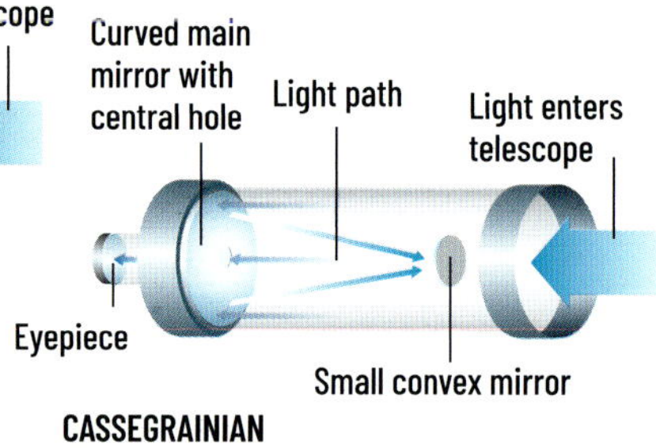

The arrangement of lenses and mirrors in refracting and reflecting telescopes.

TIMELINE
1658-1665

KEY:
Astronomy and Math
Physical and Life Sciences
Technology

1658 English scientist Robert Hooke makes a watch regulated by a hairspring, which releases the power of the main spring very gradually.

1659 Swiss mathematician Johann Rahn introduces the division sign (÷) to math.

1661 Irish scientist Robert Boyle defines chemical elements for the first time.

1661 Dutch scientist Christiaan Huygens invents the manometer, a device for measuring gas pressure.

Mirrors Instead of Lenses

These early telescopes were refracting telescopes. A better way to view images is with a reflecting telescope that uses mirrors instead of lenses, because mirrors do not cause chromatic aberration. James Gregory, a Scottish mathematician, realized this in 1663 when he published a design for a telescope that had a small, curved secondary mirror that reflected the light back through a hole in the primary mirror to an eyepiece. English scientist Robert Hooke later improved the design. Other types of reflecting telescopes were built—by Isaac Newton in 1668 and by French priest Laurent Cassegrain in 1672. (The Cassegrainian design was not perfected until 1740 by Scottish optician James Short.)

In 1857, French physicist Léon Foucault devised a method of silvering glass to make curved mirrors. They were easier to manufacture, and could be resilvered if damaged. Since then, telescopes have been made larger and more powerful—it is far easier to make a large mirror than it is to make a big lens.

William Herschel's 1794 reflecting telescope was 20 feet (6 m) long.

1662 Boyle formulates Boyle's law, which states that at a fixed temperature, the pressure of a gas is inversely proportional to its volume.

1664 English scientist Robert Hooke proposes that the planets are held in their orbits by the gravity of the sun.

1665 Robert Hooke proposes the wave theory of light, later championed by Christiaan Huygens.

1665 Hooke coins the word "cell" to describe the "little boxes" he sees in plant tissue through a microscope.

1662 1664 1665

Antonie van Leeuwenhoek

Van Leeuwenhoek was the first person to see into the world of microbes. His microscope opened up new worlds to science.

In the ancient world, some thinkers had suggested that diseases must be caused by tiny, invisible creatures moving from person to person. However, no one was able to see these life forms. It was not until the late 17th century that a world of life forms so far invisible to the naked human eye were eventually discovered.

Antonie van Leeuwenhoek, in a painting by Jan Verkolje. Van Leeuwenhoek's invitation to become a member of the London Royal Society is in front of him on the table.

Closer to Home

During the 1700s, various scientists and inventors were using glasses polished and ground in different ways to create telescopes. Van Leeuwenhoek's great breakthrough was that he used the magnifying properties of glass lenses to look at small objects, rather than objects that were far away.

Van Leeuwenhoek was born in 1632 in Delft, in the Dutch Republic, the country now known as the Netherlands. By the

TIMELINE
1665–1670

KEY:
- Astronomy and Math
- Physical and Life Sciences
- Technology

1665 The first blood transfusion, carried out by English physician Richard Lower, is performed between two dogs.

1665 Isaac Newton publishes the binomial theorem, an important concept in the development of algebra.

1666 Italian astronomer Giovanni Cassini observes the polar ice caps on Mars.

1666 French engineer Jean de Thévenot invents the spirit level.

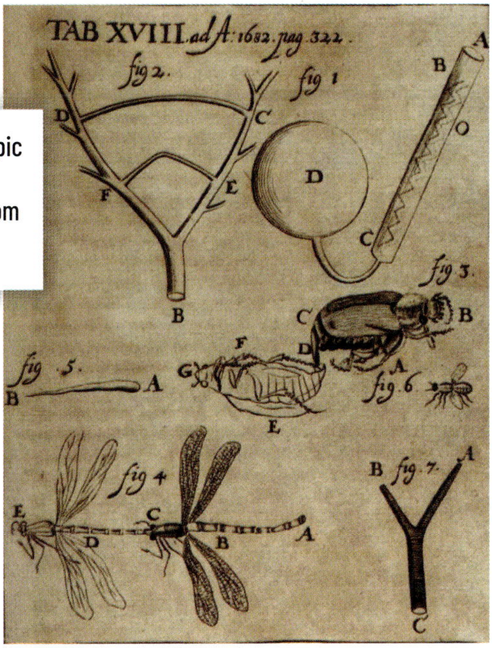

Some of the microscopic organisms that Van Leeuwenhoek drew from his observations.

time he was 10 years old, both his natural father and his stepfather had died. He became an apprentice in a draper's shop in Amsterdam, and then opened his own shop in Delft. Working hard, he became a wealthy merchant and was given various state positions.

Van Leeuwenhoek began looking at small objects through a microscope because he wanted a more detailed view of the threads in the cloth he was buying

Timeline

27 BCE Death of Roman scholar Marcus Terentius Varro, who had described how disease is carried by small organisms

1658 Jesuit priest Athanasius Kircher describes seeing small organisms in putrid meat

1666 Robert Hooke describes the fruiting bodies of mold

1673 The Royal Society receives its first letter from van Leeuwenhoek in which he describes his observations of microscopic creatures

1723 Death of Antonie van Leeuwenhoek

2021 Researchers in the Netherlands confirm that van Leeuwenhoek used heat and thin glass threads to create his best microscopes

1668 | 1669 | 1670

1668 English mathematician John Wallis proposes the law of conservation of momentum: the momentum of objects before a collision is the same as their combined momentum afterward.

1669 German alchemist Hennig Brand discovers phosphorus in urine; it is the first discovery of a new element since ancient times.

1670 French winemaker Dom Pérignon creates the first champagne.

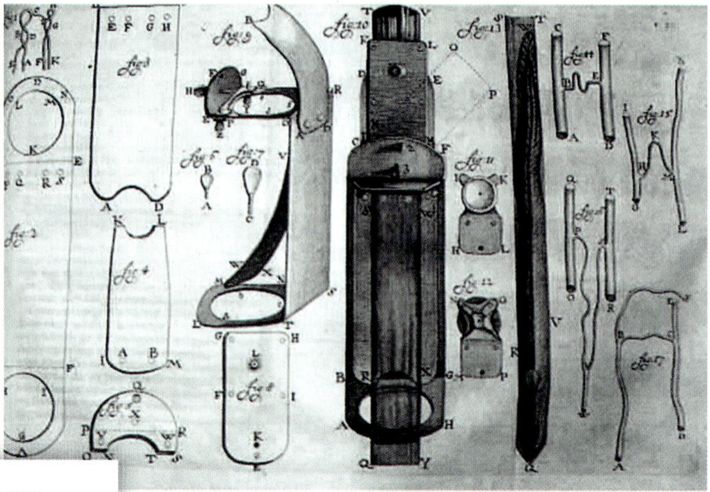

A drawing of some of van Leeuwenhoek's microscopes.

and selling. He never revealed the secret of how he made his best microscopes, and little is known about the method he used. It seems that he heated a special kind of glass in a hot flame and pulled the heated section apart to create thin filaments of glass. These gave greater magnification than it was possible to achieve by grinding lenses. However, van Leeuwenhoek was unwilling to reveal his technique and encouraged the outside world to believe that he simply ground his lenses.

The best microscopes that van Leeuwenhoek created were extremely small, just 2 inches (5 cm) long. However, they magnified objects by up to 275 times. He may also have made microscopes that magnified by 500 times, but these have not survived.

TIMELINE

1670–1675

KEY:

Astronomy and Math

Physical and Life Sciences

Technology

1670 By measuring part of the meridian (a line of longitude), French astronomer Jean Picard makes it possible to calculate the accurate circumference of Earth.

1670

1670 English doctor Thomas Willis detects sugar in the urine of patients with diabetes.

1671

1671 English scientist Isaac Newton uses a glass prism to split white light into a spectrum of colors.

A New World

The Italian biologist and physician Marcello Malpighi had used less powerful lenses to identify small blood vessels in the body. Van Leeuwenhoek showed that there was an enormous world of creatures too small for the human eye to observe. He called these creatures "animacules," and realized that they were everywhere: in water, in food, and even on his teeth.

From 1673, van Leeuwenhoek began to write a series of letters to the Royal Society in London in which he described his discoveries. In total he wrote 190 letters, all in his local Dutch dialect, which were then translated into English and Latin. In 1680, he was made a member of the Royal Society.

Now famous, van Leeuwenhoek was visited by many important people, but he showed them inferior microscopes instead of revealing his best ones. He died in 1723. After his death, other scientists began making observations using microscopes and the technology improved rapidly.

Van Leeuwenhoek knew the Delft painter Johannes Vermeer. Some people believe the man in Vermeer's painting *The Geographer* (1669) is van Leeuwenhoek.

1672 Dutch physician Jan Swammerdam identifies the human ovaries.

1673 Dutch scientist Antonie van Leeuwenhoek begins describing his observations of microscopic creatures.

1674 English glassmaker George Ravenscroft develops lead crystal glass.

1675 The Royal Greenwich Observatory is completed near London; it gives its name to the Greenwich Meridian (at longitude 0°).

1672 1673 1674 1675

The Nature of Light

Does light consist of a stream of minute particles, like bullets from a machine gun? Or does it consist of waves capable of rippling across the vast vacuum of space?

Archimedes may have used a lens to defend Syracuse against naval attack.

TIMELINE
1675–1680

KEY:

Astronomy and Math

Physical and Life Sciences

Technology

1675 Isaac Newton proposes (but does not publish) the corpuscular theory, that light travels in a series of minute particles.

1675 Italian astronomer Giovanni Cassini discovers the gap in the rings of Saturn known as the Cassini division.

1676 Van Leeuwenhoek reports his observations of bacteria through a simple, homemade microscope.

1676 Danish astronomer Ole Rømer attempts unsuccessfully to measure the speed of light.

Rays of light bend as they pass through a lens and come to a focus. Concentrating the rays allows a magnifying glass to be used as a burning glass. In 212 BCE, Greek scientist Archimedes is said to have used a burning glass to destroy the Roman ships that were attacking Syracuse, a city in Sicily.

In 1621, the Dutch mathematician Willebrord Snell measured this bending of light. Another mathematician, the Frenchman Pierre de Fermat, figured out how light casts shadows. He stated that it is because light always travels in straight lines—it will not "go around corners" to illuminate a shadow. Fermat's principle was proposed in 1640. He also observed that light travels more slowly when it passes through a denser medium.

Timeline

1621 Snell's law (refraction of light)

1640 Fermat's principle

1665 Wave theory (Hooke)

1675 Corpuscular theory (Isaac Newton)

1676 Speed of light (Rømer)

1801 Interference of light

1900 Quantum theory (Planck)

1924 Wave-particle duality

The Speed of Light

The first attempt to measure the speed of light was made in 1676 by Danish astronomer Ole

Fermat saw that shadows are formed because light travels in straight lines.

1676 Irish scientist Robert Boyle invents the hydrometer, for measuring the relative density of a liquid.

1679 German mathematician Gottfried Leibniz introduces binary arithmetic, which uses only two digits; today, binary math is used by all computers.

1680 Robert Boyle invents a match that uses a mixture of sulfur and phosphorus; it remains the basic match for over 200 years.

Snell's Law

Snell's law is named for Willebrord Snell, the Dutch mathematician who discovered it in 1621. It concerns refraction, or how a ray of light changes direction when it goes from one transparent medium to another, such as moving from air into a block of glass. The amount of refraction depends on a property of the denser medium, called its refractive index.

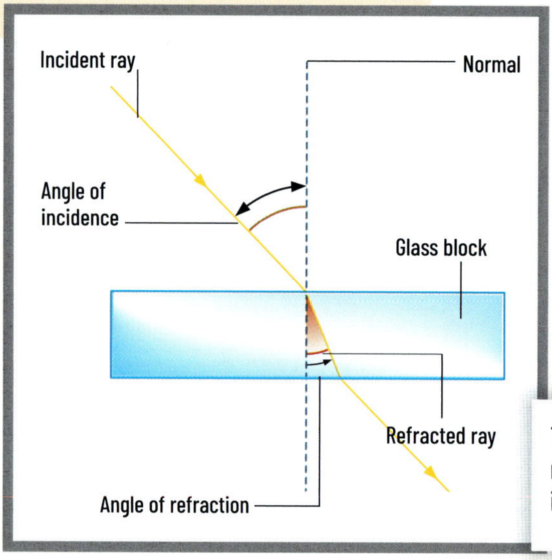

The refractive index of glass is the relationship between the angle of incidence and the angle of refraction.

Rømer. He was checking predictions about the timing of eclipses of Jupiter's moons (when they move out of sight behind the planet). Rømer discovered that the eclipses seemed to happen earlier than predicted when Earth was moving toward Jupiter and later when Earth was moving away from it. He accounted for the differences by assuming that the light had to travel a shorter or longer distance, and that light must therefore have a finite speed, which he calculated as 140,000 miles (225,000 km) per second—about 75 percent of the actual value. It was nearly 200 years before French physicist Armand Fizeau obtained a more accurate value of 195,737 miles (315,000 km) per second. The value that is used today is 186,288 miles (299,793 km) per second.

TIMELINE
1681–1687

KEY:

Astronomy and Math

Physical and Life Sciences

1681 On the island of Mauritius in the Indian Ocean, the flightless dodo (*Raphus cucullatus*) is hunted to extinction.

1682 English astronomer Edmund Halley plots the course of the comet now named for him.

1682 English botanist Nehemiah Grew describes the male and female parts of flowers.

What Is Light?

Isaac Newton believed that light travels as a stream of particles.

In 1675, English scientist Isaac Newton suggested that light travels as a stream of minute particles ("corpuscles"). Various physicists challenged this idea, the first being Robert Hooke, who had already proposed the wave theory in 1665. The final nail in the coffin of the corpuscular theory came in 1801, when English physicist Thomas Young discovered interference of light. He found that white light shining through a narrow slit is split into the colors of the rainbow. At that time it could be explained only if light was assumed to travel as waves.

The wave theory was assumed to be correct until the beginning of the 20th century, when German physicist Max Planck put forward his quantum theory. It postulates that all forms of energy, including light, travel in finite "packets," or quanta, similar to Newton's corpuscles. But in 1924, French physicist Louis de Broglie put forward the idea that moving particles can also behave like waves, as was soon proved true. So it turned out that everyone had been correct—and one of the great arguments of science melted away.

1683 English physician Thomas Sydenham gives the first full description of the condition known as gout.

1684 Japanese mathematician Seki Kowa introduces the use of determinants to math; they are useful for solving simultaneous equations.

1683 | 1684 | 1686 | 1687

1686 English naturalist John Ray proposes the word "species" to describe an interbreeding group of plants.

1687 English scientist Isaac Newton publishes his major work *Principia,* in which he sets out theories in astronomy, math, and physics.

Robert Boyle

Robert Boyle was an outstanding chemist and researcher. He also played a key role in the development of science as a founder member of Britain's Royal Society.

Robert Boyle was born in 1627. He lived much of his life through the tumult of civil war in England and Ireland. He was a wealthy aristocrat, but devoted himself to study and research, especially to the study of what we now call chemistry.

Visiting Italy

In 1641, Boyle and the personal tutor his rich family had employed began a tour of Europe. They spent some in Italy, where Boyle was disappointed not to meet Galileo Galilei, who had just died. The young Boyle was interested in the discoveries Galileo had made. Boyle returned from Europe in 1644, at the height of the political unrest of the English Civil Wars. He spent time at his family's estates in the west of

Boyle in 1689, by the German artist Johann Kerseboom. At this time Boyle lived in London, and was an important member of the Royal Society.

TIMELINE
1687–1694

KEY:

- Astronomy and Math
- Physical and Life Sciences
- Technology

1687

1687 German astronomer Gottfried Kirch discovers that Zeta Cygni is a variable star.

1687 French physicist Guillaume Amontons invents a hygrometer, for measuring the humidity of the atmosphere.

1689

1689 In Germany, Johann Denner develops the clarinet.

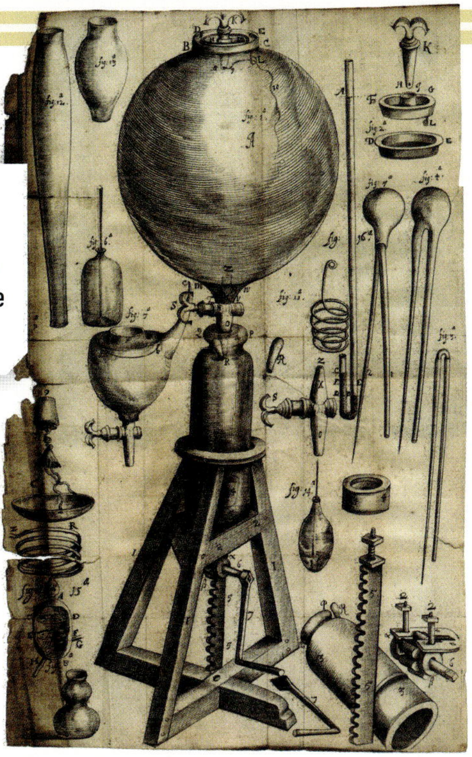

The pump for creating a vacuum by drawing air from a cylinder that Boyle invented in 1659.

Timeline

1644 Evangelista Torricelli creates a vacuum using a glass tube and a bowl of mercury

1659 Robert Boyle devises an efficient air pump to create a vacuum

1662 Devises the laws concerning gas pressure and volume that bears his name

1691 Death of Robert Boyle

1811 Avogadro's Law relates the volume of a gas in a container to the amount of substance of a gas present in the container

England and Ireland, but found it difficult to undertake the research he wanted to do in Ireland. He moved back to England in 1654 and went to Oxford.

While he was in Oxford, Boyle invented a vacuum pump in 1659 that was much more efficient than those in use at the time. Boyle's pumps created vacuums within containers, to help study the composition of gases. Boyle then went on to further the study of gases and devised

1690 English naturalist John Ray distinguishes between plants with one seed leaf (monocotyledons) and those with two (dicotyledons).

1691 John Ray suggests that fossils are the remains of creatures that lived in the distant past.

1692 The Canal du Midi is completed in France, linking the Atlantic Ocean and the Mediterranean Sea.

1694 English clockmaker Daniel Quare makes a portable barometer.

1690 1691 1692 1694

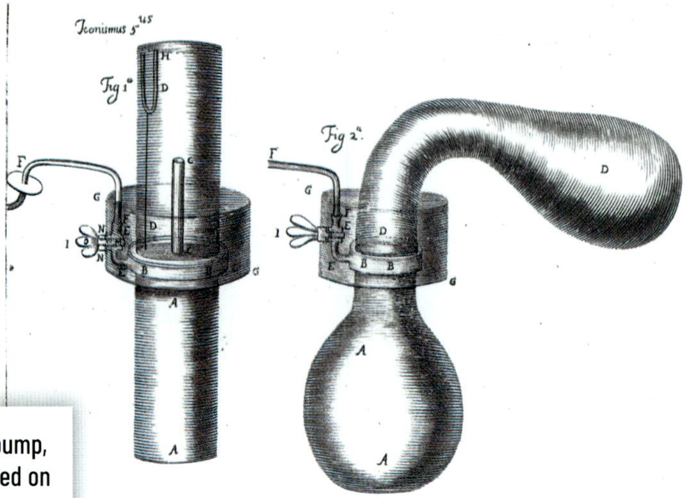

Robert Boyle's third air pump, invented in 1682, improved on his previous design.

the law of gas pressures that bears his name—"Boyle's Law." The law was published in 1662, and stated that there is relationship between the volume of a gas and the pressure it is under. This is one of the basic ideas in the study of how gases behave.

The Invisible College

Boyle was part of a group of scholars who called themselves the Invisible College. They wanted to further the study of what they called the "new philosophy"—what we would call scientific research. This group became the Royal Society in 1663, with Boyle as one of the founder members. The Royal Society of London for Improving Natural

TIMELINE

1694–1699

KEY:

Physical and Life Sciences

Technology

1694 Italian scientist Carlo Renaldini suggests that the freezing and boiling points of water should be used as fixed points on thermometers.

1694

1697

1697 German chemist George Stahl champions the (incorrect) phlogiston theory (that burning objects release a gas, phlogiston).

Knowledge, as the society was officially known, became the most important forum for the publication and debate of scientific research in the late 1600s and 1700s.

Other Interests Boyle lived in London from 1668 until his death in 1691. He shared a house with his sister Katherine, who was also a scientific researcher. Their wealth enabled them to create a laboratory, where they could experiment with various different substances. Although Boyle was in some ways the first modern chemist, he believed, in common with the medieval alchemists, that he would be able to turn cheap base metals into gold. He was also interested in religion, and wrote religious works. But he will be best remembered for his contribution to modern science.

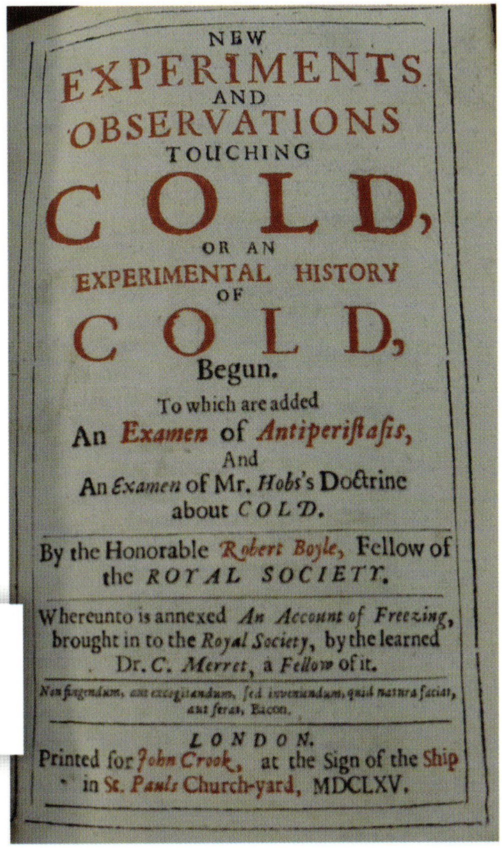
NEW
EXPERIMENTS
AND
OBSERVATIONS
TOUCHING
COLD,
OR AN
EXPERIMENTAL HISTORY
OF
COLD,
Begun.
To which are added
An Examen of Antiperistasis,
And
An Examen of Mr. Hobs's Doctrine
about COLD.
By the Honorable Robert Boyle, Fellow of the ROYAL SOCIETY.
Whereunto is annexed An Account of Freezing, brought in to the Royal Society, by the learned Dr. C. Merret, a Fellow of it.
Non fingendum, aut excogitandum, sed inveniendum, quid natura faciat, aut ferat. Bacon.
LONDON.
Printed for John Crook, at the Sign of the Ship in St. Pauls Church-yard, MDCLXV.

New Experiments and Observations Touching Cold was a 1665 work that Boyle presented to the Royal Society.

1696 1698 1699

1696 Dutch scientist Antonie van Leeuwenhoek describes "animalcules"—microorganisms today known as protists.

1698 English mining engineer Thomas Savery invents a steam pump, the forerunner of the atmospheric steam engine.

1698 The first lighthouse is built on Eddystone Rocks in the English Channel.

1699 English botanist John Woodward demonstrates that plants grow best if other substances are added to their water as nutrients.

Glossary

anatomy The scientific study of the human body.

astronomy The study of objects outside Earth's atmosphere.

concave Describes a lens that is thicker at its edges and thinner toward its center.

convex Describes a lens that bulges outward toward its center.

differential calculus An advanced branch of math.

experiment A controlled practical exercise carried out in order to test a scientific hypothesis.

geometry The study of shapes and volume.

gravity The force of attraction that exists between all objects, but usually referring to the hold of planets and other heavenly bodies.

Inquisition A religious court set up by the Catholic Church to enforce church doctrines.

lens A piece of glass that has been ground to focus beams of light together or to separate them.

movable type Wooden or metal letters that can be assembled into words, sentences, and pages for printing, then taken apart and reused.

observatory A building that houses astronomical instruments such as telescopes.

optics The scientific study of light.

reflection The angle at which a beam of light is reflected from another surface.

Reformation A period of religious reform and conflict that followed Martin Luther's criticisms of the Catholic Church in 1517 and the creation of the Protestant Church.

refraction The angle at which a beam of light changes direction when it passes from one medium to another, such as from air into glass.

Renaissance A period in European history from about 1350 to about 1550, marked by renewed interest in the Classical learning of ancient Greece and Rome.

transit A phenomenon in which one astronomical body passes in front of another, such as a planet passing in front of the sun.

Further Information

Books

Burling, Alexis. *Robert Boyle (Leaders of the Scientific Revolution).* Rosen Publishing, 2018.

Graphic Science Biographies. *Galileo Galilei and the Movement of the Planets.* Lerner Publishing Group, 2023.

Hawcock, David. *Leonardo da Vinci: Extraordinary Machines.* Dover Publications, 2019.

Wood, Alix. *Sir Isaac Newton (World-Changing Scientists).* Rosen Publishing, 2019.

Wood, Alix. *Leonardo Da Vinci (World-Changing Scientists).* Rosen Publishing, 2019.

Websites

www.biography.com/scientists/isaac-newton
Biography, inventions, and quick facts about Isaac Newton and his place in scientific history.

www.britannica.com/science/Scientific-Revolution/Physics
Pages from Britannica on the scientific revolution, with numerous links.

www.sciencemuseum.org.uk/objects-and-stories/17th-century-society-transformed-science
Information about the Royal Society, the 17th century society that transformed science.

www.thoughtco.com/17th-century-timeline-1992482
A ThoughtCo. timeline of 17th century science from 1600 to 1699, with links to key scientists and their inventions.

Index